LEVITICUS

Chapters 15—27

J. Vernon McGee

THOMAS NELSON PUBLISHERS

Nashville • Atlanta • London • Vancouver

Published in Nashville, Tennessee, by Thomas Nelson, Inc.

Scripture quotations are from the KING JAMES VERSION of the Bible.

Library of Congress Cataloging-in-Publication Data

McGee, J. Vernon (John Vernon), 1904–1988
    [Thru the Bible with J. Vernon McGee]
    Thru the Bible commentary series / J. Vernon McGee.
      p.   cm.
    Reprint. Originally published: Thru the Bible with J. Vernon
McGee. 1975.
    Includes bibliographical references.
    ISBN 0-7852-1007-5 (TR)
    ISBN 0-7852-1073-3 (NRM)
    1. Bible—Commentaries. I. Title.
BS491.2.M37 1991
220.7′7—dc20   90–41340
                                      CIP

Printed in the United States of America

5 6 7 8 9 — 99 98 97

CONTENTS

LEVITICUS—CHAPTERS 15—27

PREFACE

The radio broadcasts of the Thru the Bible Radio five-year program were transcribed, edited, and published first in single-volume paperbacks to accommodate the radio audience.

There has been a minimal amount of further editing for this publication. Therefore, these messages are not the word-for-word recording of the taped messages which went out over the air. The changes were necessary to accommodate a reading audience rather than a listening audience.

These are popular messages, prepared originally for a radio audience. They should not be considered a commentary on the entire Bible in any sense of that term. These messages are devoid of any attempt to present a theological or technical commentary on the Bible. Behind these messages is a great deal of research and study in order to interpret the Bible from a popular rather than from a scholarly (and too-often boring) viewpoint.

We have definitely and deliberately attempted "to put the cookies on the bottom shelf so that the kiddies could get them."

The fact that these messages have been translated into many languages for radio broadcasting and have been received with enthusiasm reveals the need for a simple teaching of the whole Bible for the masses of the world.

I am indebted to many people and to many sources for bringing this volume into existence. I should express my especial thanks to my secretary, Gertrude Cutler, who supervised the editorial work; to Dr. Elliott R. Cole, my associate, who handled all the detailed work with the publishers; and finally, to my wife Ruth for tenaciously encouraging me from the beginning to put my notes and messages into printed form.

Solomon wrote, ". . . of making many books there is no end; and much study is a weariness of the flesh" (Eccl. 12:12). On a sea of books that flood the marketplace, we launch this series of THRU THE BIBLE with the hope that it might draw many to the one Book, The Bible.

J. VERNON MCGEE

The Book of
LEVITICUS

INTRODUCTION

Many years ago, I read a statement by Dr. S. H. Kellogg saying that he considered the Book of Leviticus the most important book in the Bible. I felt that he must have had his tongue in cheek to make a statement like that. Then I heard a great preacher in Memphis, Tennessee, Dr. Albert C. Dudley, say that he considered the Book of Leviticus the greatest book in the Bible.

Several years ago I made an experiment on our radio program, and actually I didn't know what would happen as I began teaching this book. I wanted to study it and I wanted to see if it was such a great book, and I must confess that I had misgivings as to the value of Leviticus for a popular exposition on the Bible. However, I discovered that it is a thrilling book, and not only that, but I can now honestly say that I consider the Book of Leviticus one of the most important books of the Bible. If it were possible for me to get the message of this book into the hearts of all people who are trying to be religious, all cults and "isms" would end. A knowledge of the Book of Leviticus would accomplish that.

The Book of Leviticus was written by Moses. It is a part of the Pentateuch, the first five books of the Bible.

In the Book of Leviticus, the children of Israel were marking time at Mount Sinai. The book opens and closes at the same geographical spot, Mount Sinai, where God gave the Law. You will remember that Exodus concluded with the construction of the tabernacle according to God's instructions and then the filling of the tabernacle with the glory of the Lord. Leviticus continues by giving the order and rules of worship in the tabernacle. Leviticus is the great book on worship.

The book opens with the Hebrew word *Vayick-rah,* which means "and He called." God has now moved to the tabernacle and speaks from there; He no longer speaks from Mount Sinai. He calls the people to meet with Him at the tabernacle. He tells them how they are to come and how they are to walk before Him. The exact meaning of the church, the *ekklesia,* is the "called out ones." We are also those who have been called out. In that day, God spoke from the tabernacle and asked them to come to Him. Today, the Lord Jesus calls us to Himself. He says, "My sheep hear my voice" (John 10:27). So this book has a wonderful message for us today.

Leviticus is the book of worship. Sacrifice, ceremony, ritual, liturgy, instructions, washings, convocations, holy days, observances, conditions, and warnings crowd this book. All these physical exercises were given to teach spiritual truths. Paul wrote: "Now all these things happened unto them for ensamples: and they are written for our admonition, upon whom the ends of the world are come" (1 Cor. 10:11). In 1 Corinthians 10:6 he says, "Now these things were our examples . . .". "For whatsoever things were written aforetime were written for our learning, that we through patience and comfort of the scriptures might have hope" (Rom. 15:4).

Peter tells us that the Old Testament holds spiritual truths for us. "Of which salvation the prophets have inquired and searched diligently, who prophesied of the grace that should come unto you: Searching what, or what manner of time the Spirit of Christ which was in them did signify, when it testified beforehand the sufferings of Christ, and the glory that should follow. Unto whom it was revealed, that not unto themselves, but unto us they did minister the things, which are now reported unto you . . ." (1 Pet. 1:10–12). Hebrews 11:13 says, "These all died in faith, not having received the promises, but having seen them afar off, and were persuaded of them, and embraced them, and confessed that they were strangers and pilgrims on the earth."

Leviticus has some wonderful instruction for us today for it reveals Christ in a most remarkable manner. Tyndale, in his *Prologue into the*

Third Book of Moses, said, "Though sacrifices and ceremonies can be no ground or foundation to build upon—that is, though we can prove nought with them—yet when we have once found Christ and his mysteries, then we may borrow figures, that is to say, allegories, similitudes, and examples, to open Christ, and the secrets of God hid in Christ, even unto the quick: and can declare them more lively and sensibly with them than with all the words of the world."

Worship for us today is no longer by ritual or in a specific place. You remember that the people of Israel had been going through ceremonies and they had their rituals, but Jesus said to the woman at the well in Samaria, ". . . Woman, believe me, the hour cometh, when ye shall neither in this mountain, nor yet at Jerusalem, worship the Father. Ye worship ye know not what: we know what we worship: for salvation is of the Jews. But the hour cometh, and now is, when the true worshippers shall worship the Father in spirit and in truth: for the Father seeketh such to worship him. God is a Spirit: and they that worship him must worship him in spirit and in truth" (John 4:21–24).

The keynote to the book is holiness unto Jehovah. The message of the book is twofold:

1. Leviticus teaches that the way to God is by sacrifice. The word *atonement* occurs 45 times in this book. Atonement means to "cover up." The blood of bulls and goats did not actually take away sin. It covered over sin until Christ came to take away all sins. This is what Paul is referring to in Romans 3:25: "Whom God hath set forth to be a propitiation through faith in his blood, to declare his righteousness for the remission of sins that are past, through the forbearance of God."

The sins that are past are the sins back in the Old Testament. You see, God never accepted the blood of bulls and goats as the final payment for sin, but He required that blood be shed. It was an atonement to *cover over* the sins until Christ came. In other words, God saved "on credit" in the Old Testament. When Christ came, as the hymn accurately states it, "Jesus paid it all." This is true as far as the past is concerned, and as far as the present is concerned, and as far as the future is concerned.

One of the key verses in Leviticus, dealing with atonement, is found in Leviticus 17:11, "For the life of the flesh is in the blood: and I have given it to you upon the altar to make an atonement for your souls: for it is the blood that maketh an atonement for the soul." The way to God is by sacrifice and without the shedding of blood, there is no remission of sins.

2. Leviticus teaches that the walk with God is by sanctification. The word *holiness* occurs 87 times in this book. "And ye shall be holy unto me: for I the LORD am holy, and have severed you from other people, that ye should be mine" (Lev. 20:26).

God gave strict laws governing the diet, social life, and daily details involving every physical aspect of the lives of His people. These laws have a greater spiritual application to His people today. That is the reason I think we ought to study Leviticus. You see, access to God is secured for the sinner today through the shed blood of Christ. The writer to the Hebrews stated it this way: "Nor yet that he should offer himself often, as the high priest entereth into the holy place every year with blood of others; for then must he often have suffered since the foundation of the world: but now once in the end of the world [literally, end of the age] hath he appeared to put away sin by the sacrifice of himself" (Heb. 9:25–26).

Those who are redeemed by the blood of Christ must live a holy life if they are to enjoy and worship God. "Now the God of peace, that brought again from the dead our Lord Jesus, that great shepherd of the sheep, through the blood of the everlasting covenant, make you perfect in every good work to do his will, working in you that which is well-pleasing in his sight, through Jesus Christ; to whom be glory for ever and ever. Amen" (Heb. 13:20–21).

Leviticus is a remarkable book, as the contents are considered in the light of the New Testament. This book is about as dull as anything possibly could be to the average Christian and you won't find very many classes or individuals reading and studying the Book of Leviticus. Yet, it is a remarkable book.

1. The five offerings which open this book are clear, crystal-cut cameos of Christ. They depict His hypostatical person in depth and His death in detail (chapters 1—7).

2. The consecration of the priests reveals how shallow and in-

adequate is our thinking on Christian consecration (chapters 8—10).

3. The diet God provided for His people was sanitary and thera-peutic, and contains much spiritual food for our souls (chapter 11).

4. Attention is given to motherhood and is a further example of God's thinking concerning womanhood (chapter 12).

5. The prominence given to leprosy and its treatment, in the heart of this book on worship, demands our attention. Why is there this extended section on leprosy? Those who have been given gracious insights into Scripture have found here a type of sin and its defiling effect on man in his relation to God. The cleansing of the leper finds its fulfillment in the death and resurrection of Christ as typified in a most unusual sacrifice of two birds (chapters 13—15). My friend, if you and I would escape the defilement of sin in this world, we need to know a great deal about the death and resurrection of Christ and the application of it to our lives.

6. The great Day of Atonement is a full-length portrait of the sacrifice of Christ (chapter 16).

7. The importance of the burnt altar in the tabernacle highlights the essential characteristic of the Cross of Christ (chapter 17).

8. The emphasis in this book of instructions concerning seemingly minute details in the daily lives of God's people reveals how God intends the human family to be involved with Him (chapters 18—22). God wants to get involved in your business, in your family life, in your social life. My friend, let us beware lest we shut Him out of our lives.

9. The list of feasts furnishes a prophetic program of God's agenda for all time (chapter 23).

10. The laws governing the land of Palestine furnish an interpretation of its checkered history and an insight into its future prominence. There are a lot of prophecies in this book. The nation Israel and the Promised Land are intertwined and interwoven from here to eternity (chapters 24—27).

There is a relationship in the first three books of the Bible:

In Genesis we see man ruined.

In Exodus we see man redeemed.

In Leviticus we see man worshiping God.

We can also make a comparison and contrast between Exodus and Leviticus. In the Book of Exodus we see the offer of pardon; Leviticus offers purity. In Exodus we have God's approach to man; in Leviticus it is man's approach to God. In Exodus Christ is the Savior; in Leviticus He is the Sanctifier. In Exodus man's guilt is prominent; in Leviticus man's defilement is prominent. In Exodus God speaks out of the mount; in Leviticus He speaks out of the tabernacle. In Exodus man is made nigh to God; in Leviticus man is kept nigh to God.

OUTLINE

I. **The Five Offerings and the Law of Them, Chapters 1—7**
   A. Sweet Savor Offerings (Person of Christ), Chapters 1—3
      1. Burnt Offering (Christ Our Substitute), Chapter 1
      2. Meal Offering (Loveliness of Christ), Chapter 2
      3. Peace Offering (Christ Our Peace), Chapter 3
   B. Non-Sweet Savor Offerings (Work of Christ on Cross), Chapters 4—5
      1. Sin Offering (Sin as a Nature), Chapter 4
      2. Trespass Offering (Sin as an Act), Chapter 5
   C. Law of the Offerings, Chapters 6—7

II. **The Priests—All Believers Are Priests, Chapters 8—10**
   A. Consecration of Priests, Chapter 8
   B. Ministry of Priests, Chapter 9
   C. Restrictions on Priests; Death of Nadab and Abihu, Chapter 10

III. **Holiness in Daily Life—God Concerned with His Children's Conduct, Chapters 11—22**
   A. Food of God's People, Chapter 11
   B. Children of God's Children, Chapter 12
   C. Cleansing of Leprosy, Chapters 13—14
   D. Cleansing of Running Issues, Chapter 15
   E. Great Day of Atonement, Chapter 16
   F. Place of Sacrifice; Value of the Blood, Chapter 17
   G. Application of Commandments to Life Situations, Chapters 18—20
      1. Immorality Condemned (Amplification of Seventh Commandment), Chapter 18
      2. Social Sins (Application of Commandments), Chapter 19
      3. Penalty for Breaking Commandments, Chapter 20
   H. Law for Personal Purity of the Priests, Chapters 21—22

CHAPTER 15

THEME: Running issues of the man; running issues of the woman; repulsiveness and regulations of running issues

We have had two chapters on this matter of leprosy, and that has been bad enough, but it is going to get worse in this chapter. We are hearing a great deal about the pollution of our ecology in these days but there is a pollution of our souls also, and of our minds—of our entire beings. These running sores are highly contagious and infectious, and they reveal to us the exceeding sinfulness of sin. Human nature is an overflowing cesspool and a sewer of uncleanness. Not only is human nature defiled, but it is defiling; not only is it corrupt, but it is corrupting. This chapter holds up the mirror to human nature, and after one look, no flesh can glory in His sight.

One would think that leprosy was the worst of the diseases, but actually it was not as contagious and contaminating as running issues. I would like to quote Dr. Leiker who is an authority on leprosy. "Leprosy is caused by tiny germs called leprosy bacilli, which can be seen only through a microscope. The bacilli were discovered in 1873 by the Norwegian doctor, Hansen. That is why leprosy is sometimes called Hansen's disease. The bacilli are present in large numbers in the skin of certain types of leprosy patients. They pass from these patients to the skin of healthy people, mainly by bodily contact. They then enter the skin through tiny wounds and scratches, where they may live and multiply. Only infectious patients—those who have many bacilli in their skin—are able to spread the disease. Many patients have no bacilli left in their skin and therefore they do not pass on the disease.

"Frequent bathing, washing of clothes, and keeping a clean house will help to prevent the disease, because many bacilli can be washed away with water and soap before they enter the skin. The most important thing is to avoid bodily contact with infectious cases of leprosy.

The germs are not carried by air or by insects. There is no proof that leprosy is spread in other ways, but it may be that the disease is spread occasionally by means other than bodily contact.

"You may use patients' clothes, sleeping mats, tools, and so on, without risk, provided they are washed with hot water and soap and have been in the sun for at least 24 hours. There is no danger in visiting patients' homes, or even in shaking hands with them, but you should wash your hands afterwards. There is no reason to fear leprosy if these simple safeguards are taken."

Leprosy was a disease that could not be kept a secret for long. It worked slowly, but it would finally break out. In contrast, running issues could be kept secret for a lifetime. These represent the thought life of man as well as the overt act of sin. "And God saw that the wickedness of man was great in the earth, and that every imagination of the thoughts of his heart was only evil continually" (Gen. 6:5). This has to do with that part of human nature that is defiled and affects others. "Who can bring a clean thing out of an unclean? not one" (Job 14:4). "Who can understand his errors? cleanse thou me from secret faults" (Ps. 19:12). "For I know that in me (that is, in my flesh,) dwelleth no good thing: for to will is present with me; but how to perform that which is good I find not" (Rom. 7:18). Here we have the nature of man that is hidden. No one else may know about it. This is what we know down deep in our hearts. Yet, this secret sin can be passed on to others.

Some famous men have commented on the secret sin of man: "I see no fault committed which I too might not have committed" (Goethe). "Every man knows that of himself which he dares not tell to his dearest friends" (Dr. Samuel Johnson). "I do not know what the heart of a villain may be—I only know that of a virtuous man, and that is frightful" (Count de Maistre). "Go to your own bosom. Knock there: and ask your heart what it doth know" (Shakespeare). "Why is there no man who *confesses* his vices? It is because he has not yet laid them aside. It is a *waking* man only who can tell his dreams" (Seneca).

The curse of sin has affected man's power in the propagation of the race. Man is only capable of producing after his kind—a sinner as he is. The very fountain of the race is polluted. Many of these running issues are connected with the generative organs of the race. For the most part, they are the social diseases. There is filthiness and defilement connected with sexual sins that is appalling. David cried out to God, "Purge me with hyssop, and I shall be clean: wash me, and I shall be whiter than snow. . . . Create in me a clean heart, O God; and renew a right spirit within me" (Ps. 51:7, 10).

Today people talk about the new morality. It is interesting that they turn out the same old diseases with the new morality. Today the social diseases, venereal diseases, are increasing at an alarming rate. They are of epidemic proportion both in this country and in places abroad where our soldiers are stationed. That is the way sin is. And it robs a person of the joy of his salvation.

It seems strange that God would talk so much about such a repulsive subject. However, He gives to man a comprehensive view of the exceeding sinfulness of sin. We get an unusual view of it in this chapter. We need to recall the words of Paul, "For whatsoever things were written aforetime were written for our learning, that we through patience and comfort of the scriptures might have hope" (Rom. 15:4).

RUNNING ISSUES OF THE MAN

And the LORD spake unto Moses and to Aaron, saying [Lev. 15:1].

God addressed both Moses and Aaron. In chapter 14 where the "law of the leper" was under consideration, only the law-giver Moses was addressed. Aaron, as the high priest, is a prophetic picture of our Great High Priest. Only the Lord Jesus can give comfort and understanding to the afflicted as well as the extending of mercy and grace. Our High Priest cannot be touched by our sin, but He can be touched with the feeling of our infirmities, because He was in all points tempted as we are, yet without sin (Heb. 4:14–15 and Heb. 2:17–18).

Speak unto the children of Israel, and say unto them, When any man hath a running issue out of his flesh, because of his issue he is unclean.

**And this shall be his uncleanness in his issue: whether
his flesh run with his issue, or his flesh be stopped from
his issue, it is his uncleanness [Lev. 15:2–3].**

This vivid language reveals how sickening, disgusting, abhorrent, offensive, impure, repugnant, and utterly corrupt and corrupting the
human nature is. The pus of sin is flowing from the human heart. We
can see it all around us and in us. The defilement is here. We cannot
rub shoulders with each other without it affecting our lives because
human nature is not only corrupt, it is corrupting. You and I influence
one another. I live my life in you, and you live your life in me. It cannot be otherwise. You are a preacher, whether you know it or not. You
are preaching by your life.

When I was a pastor in Pasadena, I knew a very godly woman
whose son was a drunkard. They lived a little way from the church.
One could always tell when he was on what is called a "toot" because
he would use both sides of the street on the way home. His mother was
distressed and ashamed, and she asked me to talk with him. One day I
saw him weaving down the street and I brought him into my study to
talk with him. I told him how low-down he was, called him a sinner
and a disgrace. I called him everything you could possibly call such a
man, and he just hung his head and took it all. Then I said, "Don't you
know that you are preaching by your life?" He asked, "Are you calling
me a preacher?" When I told him he was, he got up the best he could
as drunk as he was and wanted to fight me. You could call him anything else in the world but a preacher!

Well, my friend, whoever you are, you are a preacher. You are
preaching some message by your life. You are influencing someone.

Human nature is corrupting because it is sinful. Even the regener-
ated man still carries his old sinful flesh. Listen to the words of the
Lord Jesus:

"But those things which proceed out of the mouth come forth from
the heart; and they defile the man. For out of the heart proceed evil
thoughts, murders, adulteries, fornications, thefts, false witness, blas-
phemies: These are the things which defile a man: but to eat with
unwashen hands defileth not a man" (Matt. 15:18–20).

It is amazing today how many people are interested in religious ceremonies. Even though they go through those religious ceremonies, they have a heart that is just as filthy as it possibly can be. We all have that kind of heart, unless it has been cleansed by the blood of Christ.

James makes it very practical. "But every man is tempted, when he is drawn away of his own lust, and enticed. Then when lust hath conceived, it bringeth forth . . . death" (James 1:14–15). Paul cried out in despair, ". . . I know that in me (that is, in my flesh,) dwelleth no good thing . . ." (Rom. 7:18). The sore of sin may be visible or invisible; it may be oozing blood and pus, or it may not appear on the surface, yet it is there. The uncleanness in view here is in the thought life and the secret sins—secret to man but open before God. "Behold, thou desirest truth in the inward parts: and in the hidden part thou shalt make me to know wisdom" (Ps. 51:6). This passage should humble the proud man and show how utterly disgusting he is in the light of God's presence. Listen to David: "Against thee, thee only, have I sinned, and done this evil in thy sight: that thou mightest be justified when thou speakest, and be clear when thou judgest" (Ps. 51:4).

God has emphasized in His Word again and again that sin is exceedingly sinful. Read Ezekiel 16:1–13 in which God makes it very clear to Israel that they had no virtues or attractions but were utterly disgusting to Him. They were polluted and their genealogy was bad. Or read the entire chapter of Isaiah 59, where he says, "But your iniquities have separated between you and your God, and your sins have hid his face from you, that he will not hear" (v. 2)

Every bed, whereon he lieth that hath the issue, is unclean: and every thing, whereon he sitteth, shall be unclean.

And whosoever toucheth his bed shall wash his clothes, and bathe himself in water, and be unclean until the even.

And he that sitteth on any thing whereon he sat that hath the issue shall wash his clothes, and bathe himself in water, and be unclean until the even.

> And he that toucheth the flesh of him that hath the issue
> shall wash his clothes, and bathe himself in water, and
> be unclean until the even [Lev. 15:4–7].

Everything he sits on, everything he touches is unclean.

God is concerned with the personal life of His people. His law reaches into the minute areas of their lives. He even watches over them while they are asleep! The man with an unclean issue contaminated the bed upon which he slept, and even his dreams were impure. Many a person spends a sleepless night, not counting sheep, but recalling his sins with lustful pleasure. God is interested in what we think when we lie upon our pillows. He wants to control our thought life. "Finally, brethren, whatsoever things are true, whatsoever things are honest, whatsoever things are just, whatsoever things are pure, whatsoever things are lovely, whatsoever things are of good report; if there be any virtue, and if there be any praise, think on these things" (Phil. 4:8).

God is interested in you! He is interested in you when you lie down and when you walk about. He is interested in what you touch. When we sit upon a chair in social conversation, God is interested in our conversation. Do we spread the virus of contamination? Also God is interested in our business and social contacts. Physical contact of the clean with the unclean always spreads the disease to the clean.

My friend, we cannot be with people or even just walk down the street without becoming soiled. We hear four-letter words, we see pictures, we are lured by advertising and propaganda. We are constantly soiled. We need to be aware of this and to confess our sin and to be cleansed by God. We all have this leprosy of sin, these running sores, these hidden sins.

> And if he that hath the issue spit upon him that is clean;
> then he shall wash his clothes, and bathe himself in wa-
> ter, and be unclean until the even.

> And what saddle soever he rideth upon that hath the
> issue shall be unclean.

> And whosoever toucheth any thing that was under him shall be unclean until the even: and he that beareth any of those things shall wash his clothes, and bathe himself in water, and be unclean until the even.
>
> And whomsoever he toucheth that hath the issue, and hath not rinsed his hands in water, he shall wash his clothes, and bathe himself in water, and be unclean until the even.
>
> And the vessel of the earth, that he toucheth which hath the issue, shall be broken: and every vessel of wood shall be rinsed in water [Lev. 15:8–12].

This gets down to where a person almost feels disgusted, but it reveals the nastiness of sin by contact. The former regulations had to do with conduct in the home and now this pertains to contact on the street or in a public place. Some of this we might call accidental contact.

We find this today. A believer often finds himself in a public place or on the street and some vile, dirty-minded person opens his mouth and spews out undiluted profanity and unspeakable blasphemy. This is contaminating. A believer may feel dirty after leaving such a group, and he is dirty. He needs to wash himself. That is the reason it is so very important for us to stay in the Word of God. "Wherewithal shall a young man cleanse his way? by taking heed thereto according to thy word" (Ps. 119:9). We get dirty in this life!

Listen to these words of Jesus: ". . . If I wash thee not, thou hast no part with me" (John 13:8). This means we cannot have fellowship with the Lord Jesus if we are not washed by Him. "Now ye are clean through the word which I have spoken unto you" (John 15:3). "Sanctify them through thy truth: thy word is truth" (John 17:17).

> And when he that hath an issue is cleansed of his issue; then he shall number to himself seven days for his cleansing, and wash his clothes, and bathe his flesh in running water, and shall be clean.

> And on the eighth day he shall take to him two turtle-doves, or two young pigeons, and come before the LORD unto the door of the tabernacle of the congregation, and give them unto the priest:
>
> And the priest shall offer them, the one for a sin offering, and the other for a burnt offering; and the priest shall make an atonement for him before the LORD for his issue [Lev. 15:13–15].

Here, again, we have both the water and the blood introduced. The blood removes the guilt of sin and the water removes the stain of sin. The Holy Spirit must apply the sacrifice of Christ to those secret sins which are in our lives today.

Friend, do you see what this is describing? It is a sordid chapter, and yet we must confess that it is a picture of you and me. We need to confess and be cleansed of our secret sins. "I acknowledged my sin unto thee, and mine iniquity have I not hid. I said, I will confess my transgressions unto the LORD; and thou forgavest the iniquity of my sin" (Ps. 32:5). "If we confess our sins, he is faithful and just to forgive us our sins, and to cleanse us from all unrighteousness" (1 John 1:9).

> And if any man's seed of copulation go out from him, then he shall wash all his flesh in water, and be unclean until the even.
>
> And every garment, and every skin, whereon is the seed of copulation, shall be washed with water, and be unclean until the even.
>
> The woman also with whom man shall lie with seed of copulation, they shall both bathe themselves in water, and be unclean until the even [Lev. 15:16–18].

It is obvious that this is referring to venereal diseases. Today these diseases are like an epidemic. God guards against these social diseases. God is interested in the procreation of the race. God gave this gift to man for his good and inspiration, and so guards this system carefully. Man is always in danger of debasing himself in that which was to be one of the noblest experiences.

Our Lord teaches that unholy desires and lustful thoughts are to be avoided, for they are sin. "Ye have heard that it was said by them of old time, Thou shalt not commit adultery: But I say unto you, That whosoever looketh on a woman to lust after her hath committed adultery with her already in his heart" (Matt. 5:27–28).

RUNNING ISSUE OF THE WOMAN

And if a woman have an issue, and her issue in her flesh be blood, she shall be put apart seven days: and whosoever toucheth her shall be unclean until the even.

And every thing that she lieth upon in her separation shall be unclean: every thing also that she sitteth upon shall be unclean.

And whosoever toucheth her bed shall wash his clothes, and bathe himself in water, and be unclean until the even.

And whosoever toucheth any thing that she sat upon shall wash his clothes, and bathe himself in water, and be unclean until the even.

And if it be on her bed, or on any thing whereon she sitteth, when he toucheth it, he shall be unclean until the even.

And if any man lie with her at all, and her flowers be upon him, he shall be unclean seven days; and all the bed whereon he lieth shall be unclean [Lev. 15:19–24].

These verses evidently refer to the uncleanness of a woman during her normal menstrual period. She was separated from her friends and her loved ones during this period. She was treated as an outcast and a leper (Num. 5:2). This seems to be unusually severe. The only explanation we have to offer is that this is a reminder of the fall of man as recorded in Genesis. The penalty was death. Man is reminded that he had a bad beginning and has nothing in which to glory. Sinful man can produce only sin.

> **And if a woman have an issue of her blood many days out of the time of her separation, or if it run beyond the time of her separation; all the days of the issue of her uncleanness shall be as the days of her separation: she shall be unclean.**
>
> **Every bed whereon she lieth all the days of her issue shall be unto her as the bed of her separation: and whatsoever she sitteth upon shall be unclean, as the uncleanness of her separation.**
>
> **And whosoever toucheth those things shall be unclean, and shall wash his clothes, and bathe himself in water, and be unclean until the even.**
>
> **But if she be cleansed of her issue, then she shall number to herself seven days, and after that she shall be clean.**
>
> **And on the eighth day she shall take unto her two turtles, or two young pigeons, and bring them unto the priest, to the door of the tabernacle of the congregation [Lev. 15:25–29].**

This section deals with an abnormal issue. This gives rules for her separation and the fact that she contaminates the bed she lies on and anyone who touches the things which she contaminates. It also explains the offering she is to bring when she is cleansed of her issue.

This gives us some insight into the plight of the woman with the issue of blood who came to Christ for healing (Luke 8:43–48). The Law had shut her out from contact with others, yet she touched Jesus.

The Law had shut her out from the temple and from the public worship of God. The grace of our Lord healed her and restored her, and He commended her faith. Jesus is the fountain for the cleansing of the uncleanness of our hearts.

REPULSIVENESS AND REGULATIONS
OF RUNNING ISSUES

Thus shall ye separate the children of Israel from their uncleanness; that they die not in their uncleanness, when they defile my tabernacle that is among them.

This is the law of him that hath an issue, and of him whose seed goeth from him, and is defiled therewith;

And of her that is sick of her flowers, and of him that hath an issue, of the man, and of the woman, and of him that lieth with her that is unclean [Lev. 15:31–33].

Sexual sins are obviously under primary consideration in the closing verses of the chapter concerning running issues. It is referring to venereal disease, and death was the penalty for the failure to obey the commandments regulating running issues.

Hidden sin is not a trivial matter to God. Neither does He ignore the secret sins of believers. "Know ye not that ye are the temple of God, and that the Spirit of God dwelleth in you? If any man defile the temple of God, him shall God destroy; for the temple of God is holy, which temple ye are" (1 Cor. 3:16–17). We belong to God and we are the temple of the Holy Spirit. Abuse of that temple can be a sin unto death. There is a sin unto death. "If any man see his brother sin a sin which is not unto death, he shall ask, and he shall give him life for them that sin not unto death. There is a sin unto death: I do not say that he shall pray for it" (1 John 5:16). It is possible for a believer to commit a sin so that God takes him home. There is no use praying for him, because God is going to take him home. How do you know what that sin is? You don't know. But we are to remember that God deals with His own children in judgment when that is necessary. That does not mean that everyone who dies is taken home under judgment. Yet, there is a sin unto death and God calls His children home when they continue to be disobedient. The disobedience may be in the area of secret sins.

A mother may warn her little boy not to fight with the boy next door. She tells him that if they can't play without fighting, he must come into the house. She may issue this warning several times and each time she finds him fighting. Finally, she goes out and gets precious little Willie and leads him into the house. Little Willie says, "Mama, I don't want to come in," but into the house he goes! He doesn't want to come in, but neither will he obey. God is a good disciplinarian, by the way. Sometimes a child of His keeps on sinning and commits a sin unto death; so the Father just takes him on home.

"But your iniquities have separated between you and your God, and your sins have hid his face from you, that he will not hear" (Isa. 59:2). The child of God needs to recognize this and he needs to confess his sin. There can be secret sins which the believer does not confess. If, then, God strikes him down, let us not blame God for it. The blame lies with the individual.

We are living in an age that has gone mad over sex. Sexual sins are rampant and venereal disease is becoming an epidemic. What a lesson we have in this chapter. I'm glad to close the page on this chapter because it is such an ugly picture. Yet, it is the picture of the human family and we are part of that family.

We will come now to the sixteenth chapter and it is like going out of darkness into light. We have come out of a tunnel and will enter the clear noonday sun.

CHAPTER 16

THEME: The great Day of Atonement—preparation of the priest; preparation of the place; preparation of the people

This chapter holds the greatest spiritual lesson for us. The subjects treated so far in Leviticus have been offerings, priests, and sin. None of these have dealt finally and completely with sin. We now come to that which more completely than any other deals with the subject of sin. It at least points more specifically and adequately to the work of Christ in redemption. It is a shadow of His redemptive work.

"Let no man therefore judge you in meat, or in drink, or in respect of an holyday, or of the new moon, or of the sabbath days: Which are a shadow of things to come; but the body is of Christ" (Col. 2:16–17). A shadow is a picture. Although a picture is a poor substitute for the real thing or the real person, it points to the reality. Years ago Hengstenberg commented, "The elucidation of the doctrine of types, now entirely neglected, is an important problem of future theologians." The picture, or type, of this great Day of Atonement merits our careful study.

Dr. Kellogg states the significance of the great Day of Atonement in this fashion: "[It] was perhaps the most important and characteristic in the whole Mosaic legislation." The rabbis designated the Day of Atonement with the simple word *Yoma,* "The Day." It was on this day that sin was dealt with in a more adequate way than in any other ceremony of the Mosaic system.

Notice in verse 16, ". . . and because of their transgressions in all their sins." Then in verse 22, "And the goat shall bear upon him all their iniquities . . ." and in verse 21, ". . . and confess over him all the iniquities of the children of Israel. . . ." He will make atonement for all their transgressions, all their iniquities, all their sins! This was the best that the Law had to offer until Christ should come.

The instructions and restrictions of this day grew out of the historical incident of the rebellion and disobedience of Nadab and Abihu, sons of Aaron, when they intruded into the Holy of Holies of the taber-nacle, and were immediately put to death by the direct judgment of God (chapter 10). Some writers treat these two chapters together.

The Day of Atonement was observed in the seventh month and on the tenth day. These numbers are significant in most of Scripture. The seventh is the sabbatic month and denotes rest and cessation from works. Surely it is not amiss that this month was chosen to set forth the rest of redemption that is in Christ. "For he that is entered into his rest, he also hath ceased from his own works, as God did from his" (Heb. 4:10).

Ten is another prominent number in Scripture, and seems to con-vey the idea of that which expresses God's complete will and way. There were the Ten Commandments—God could have given another, but He did not. God requested the tithe, the tenth, and the remnant of Israel is defined as a tenth (Isa. 6:13). Ten expresses God's mind and purpose. The tenth day expresses the truth that Christ came to do the will of God. It pleased the Lord to bruise Him, He hath put Him to grief. He came in the fullness of time, at the appointed hour.

The word for "atonement" is the Hebrew *kaphar,* which means "to cover." God did not take away sins in the Old Testament; He covered them until Christ came and removed them. There are a number of Scriptures which teach this. "And the times of this ignorance God winked at [overlooked]; but now commandeth all men every where to repent" (Acts 17:30). "Being justified freely by his grace through the redemption that is in Christ Jesus: Whom God hath set forth to be a propitiation [that is, a mercy seat] through faith in his blood, to de-clare his righteousness for the remission of sins that are past, through the forbearance of God" (Rom. 3:24–25). "And for this cause he is the mediator of the new testament, that by means of death, for the redemption of the transgressions that were under the first testament, they which are called might receive the promise of eternal inheri-tance" (Heb. 9:15). "The Holy Ghost this signifying, that the way into the holiest of all was not yet made manifest, while as the first taber-nacle was yet standing: Which was a figure for the time then present, in which were offered both gifts and sacrifices, that could not make him that did the service perfect, as pertaining to the conscience" (Heb. 9:8–9).

The Day of Atonement pointed to Christ and His redemption as did no other sacrifice, ceremony, or ordinance of the Old Testament. It reveals Christ, as our Great High Priest, going into the Holy of Holies for us.

PREPARATION OF THE PRIEST

And the Lord spake unto Moses after the death of the two sons of Aaron, when they offered before the Lord, and died;

And the Lord said unto Moses, Speak unto Aaron thy brother, that he come not at all times into the holy place within the vail before the mercy seat, which is upon the ark; that he die not: for I will appear in the cloud upon the mercy seat [Lev. 16:1–2].

The instructions, ordinances, and rituals for the great Day of Atonement were made essential after the incident of the death of Nadab and Abihu, who intruded into the Holy Place and were slain by the direct judgment of God. The great Day of Atonement offered an explanation for the sudden death of these two men. The utter holiness of God and the utter sinfulness of man are made clear in this service.

There is a great gulf between God and man, but it is not fixed. Thank God for that! It has been bridged. Today God offers encouragement to man to come to Him but, my friend, you must come God's way. When you come God's way, you can come with boldness. "Having therefore, brethren, boldness to enter into the holiest by the blood of Jesus, by a new and living way, which he hath consecrated for us, through the veil, that is to say, his flesh; And having an high priest over the house of God; Let us draw near with a true heart in full assurance of faith, having our hearts sprinkled from an evil conscience, and our bodies washed with pure water" (Heb. 10:19–22). "For through him [Christ Jesus] we both have access by one Spirit unto the Father" (Eph. 2:18). The invitation is to *come*. That means we are to come God's way. If we do, then we can come with great assurance.

You will notice that all this was done because these two sons of Aaron had intruded into the Holy of Holies. God now says, "You can't at all times come into My place." For us today it is different. We can come any time and any place and enter into the presence of God; that is, provided we come through Christ.

I actually think it is sinful for some people to pray. A minister who rejects Christ and who prays publicly to God, but does not come to God through Jesus Christ is coming to God in some other way which God will not accept. That is the son of Nadab and Abihu.

> **Thus shall Aaron come into the holy place: with a young bullock for a sin offering, and a ram for a burnt offering.**
>
> **He shall put on the holy linen coat, and he shall have the linen breeches upon his flesh, and shall be girded with a linen girdle, and with the linen mitre shall he be attired: these are holy garments; therefore shall he wash his flesh in water, and so put them on [Lev. 16:3–4].**

The unique and significant feature about this day was that the high priest alone performed the ritual. He had no assistance whatsoever. "And there shall be no man in the tabernacle of the congregation when he goeth in to make an atonement in the holy place . . ." (v. 17). It was all his work, from the menial tasks to the high priestly offers. All the other priests retired from the tabernacle. He alone entered, for the work of atonement was his.

This is important to see because he pictured Christ. Christ was alone with the sins of the world. "My God, my God, why hast thou forsaken me? why art thou so far from helping me, and from the words of my roaring?" (Ps. 22:1). Christ was forsaken of both God and man when He was made sin for us. Nevertheless, He and the Father were in fellowship regarding the plan of salvation. "Behold, the hour cometh, yea, is now come, that ye shall be scattered, every man to his own, and shall leave me alone: and yet I am not alone, because the Father is with me" (John 16:32). This is a great mystery. ". . . God was in Christ, reconciling the world unto himself . . ." (2 Cor. 5:19).

The high priest laid aside his garments of glory and beauty. He became attired in the same linen garb as the other priests. He washed himself and put on the linen garments only. He must be unadorned but pure.

This is a beautiful foreshadowing of Christ, our High Priest, who laid aside His glory and took upon Himself human flesh to die on the Cross. "In the beginning was the Word, and the Word was with God, and the Word was God. . . . And the Word was made flesh, and dwelt among us, (and we beheld his glory, the glory as of the only begotten of the Father,) full of grace and truth. . . . No man hath seen God at any time; the only begotten Son, which is in the bosom of the Father, he hath declared him" (John 1:1, 14, 18). Our LORD did not lay aside His deity, but He put aside His glory when He came down to this earth and became a man. "Let this mind be in you, which was also in Christ Jesus: Who, being in the form of God, thought it not robbery to be equal with God: But made himself of no reputation, and took upon him the form of a servant, and was made in the likeness of men: And being found in fashion as a man, he humbled himself, and became obedient unto death, even the death of the cross" (Phil. 2:5–8).

And he shall take of the congregation of the children of Israel two kids of the goats for a sin offering, and one ram for a burnt offering.

And Aaron shall offer his bullock of the sin offering, which is for himself, and make an atonement for himself, and for his house [Lev. 16:5–6].

This gives the final personal preparation of Aaron for this all-important day. Aaron offered a sin offering for himself and his family and maybe included the entire tribe of Levi.

This phase of the great Day of Atonement finds no counterpart in the life and work of Christ. He had no sin. He was without sin. He did not die for Himself. He was made sin for us. He never made an offering for Himself. The offering of turtledoves which was brought to the temple when He was a baby was for the cleansing of Mary, His mother. It was to remind her that she was a sinner. There is no record of a sacrifice or an offering for Jesus. But Aaron had to make an offering for himself first, and then he could make an offering for the people.

PREPARATION OF THE PLACE

And he shall take the two goats, and present them before the Lord at the door of the tabernacle of the congregation.

And Aaron shall cast lots upon the two goats; one lot for the Lord, and the other lot for the scapegoat.

And Aaron shall bring the goat upon which the Lord's lot fell, and offer him for a sin offering.

But the goat, on which the lot fell to be the scapegoat, shall be presented alive before the Lord, to make an atonement with him, and to let him go for a scapegoat into the wilderness.

And Aaron shall bring the bullock of the sin offering, which is for himself, and shall make an atonement for himself, and for his house, and shall kill the bullock of the sin offering which is for himself:

And he shall take a censer full of burning coals of fire from off the altar before the Lord, and his hands full of sweet incense beaten small, and bring it within the vail:

And he shall put the incense upon the fire before the Lord, that the cloud of the incense may cover the mercy seat that is upon the testimony, that he die not:

And he shall take of the blood of the bullock, and sprinkle it with his finger upon the mercy seat eastward; and

before the mercy seat shall he sprinkle of the blood with his finger seven times [Lev. 16:7–14].

It is well to note here that the two goats constituted one sin offering. Each presented a distinct aspect of the remission of sin. One was offered as a sin offering. The other was taken into the wilderness.

The goat sent into the wilderness was called the scapegoat. The Hebrew word is *lo-azazel*. There has been some confusion as to its meaning. The word applies primarily to the goat and its destination into the wilderness. The view of the Septuagint, Luther, Kellogg, and Andrew Bonar is that it means an entire and utter removal. Edersheim gives it the meaning, "wholly to go away." It is definitely a part of the sin offering. One lot fell on the goat to be sent away and one lot fell on the goat to be offered.

Before anything was done to the goats, Aaron had to enter the Holy of Holies with the blood of the bullock for himself and for his house. So it is not exactly accurate to say that the high priest went in only one time. He went in on only one day of the year, but he went in twice on that day.

The brazen altar was in the outer court. The bullock for his sin offering would be slain as in any other sin offering. Something new is added at the conclusion of the offering. On the way into the Holy of Holies, as he passed the laver, I am confident that he washed his hands and his feet. Then, in the Holy Place, he was to take a censer full of burning coals of fire from the golden altar of incense and with his hands full of sweet incense, he would place the incense upon the coals in the censer. When he passed the veil into the Holy of Holies, the cloud of smoke would fill the Holy of Holies. The ark and the mercy seat were in the Holy of Holies. He would take the blood of the bullock which he had brought in a basin with him, dip his finger into it, and sprinkle it before the mercy seat seven times. The blood made the top of the box a *mercy* seat. Seven times denotes a complete and adequate atonement.

I'm sure this was an awesome day for the high priest. He must perform accurately and meticulously in the presence of God. The slightest deviation would mean instant death. He probably rehearsed the ritual many times before the performance actually took place. As far as we know, no high priest ever died in the Holy of Holies. The only two who died were Nadab and Abihu.

Christ was made sin for us on the Cross. This is the counterpart to the brazen altar in the tabernacle. Then, as our Great High Priest, He entered into heaven and offered His own blood for our sins. Now the throne of God is a mercy seat for us. All of this is clearly taught us in Hebrews 9 and 10. Whereas Aaron went with fear and trembling, we are bidden to come with boldness according to Hebrews 4:16. Where he did not dare linger and could come only one day in the year, we are bidden to come constantly. Christ, our High Priest, carried His own blood and the sweet incense of His own intercession into heaven, and He is there today at God's right hand.

After Aaron had gone in for himself and his house, he was to go into the Holy of Holies for the people.

> **Then shall he kill the goat of the sin offering, that is for the people, and bring his blood within the vail, and do with that blood as he did with the blood of the bullock, and sprinkle it upon the mercy seat, and before the mercy seat:**

> **And he shall make an atonement for the holy place, because of the uncleanness of the children of Israel, and because of their transgressions in all their sins: and so shall he do for the tabernacle of the congregation, that remaineth among them in the midst of their uncleanness.**

> **And there shall be no man in the tabernacle of the congregation when he goeth in to make an atonement in the holy place, until he come out, and have made an atonement for himself, and for his household, and for all the congregation of Israel.**

> **And he shall go out unto the altar that is before the LORD, and make an atonement for it; and shall take of**

the blood of the bullock, and of the blood of the goat, and put it upon the horns of the altar round about.

And he shall sprinkle of the blood upon it with his finger seven times, and cleanse it, and hallow it from the uncleanness of the children of Israel [Lev. 16:15–19].

Now he is going in, not only for himself and his family, but for the children of Israel. This is done because of their transgressions and because of their uncleanness. The same ritual is followed in slaying the goat as in the slaying of the bullock for Aaron. He goes into the Holy of Holies as before, but now the atonement covers the Holy Place itself because of the contamination of Israel. Even the brazen altar itself must have the blood applied because this is where the sins of Israel were confessed and atoned; it is polluted because of the sin of the people.

All of this is to remind us of the One who died on the Cross for us. It is not the Cross that is important; the importance is in the One who died on the Cross. "Forasmuch as ye know that ye were not redeemed with corruptible things, as silver and gold, from your vain conversation received by tradition from your fathers; but with the precious blood of Christ, as of a lamb without blemish and without spot" (1 Pet. 1:18–19).

All of this revealed the inadequacy of the ritual of the blood of bulls and goats. "It was therefore necessary that the patterns of things in the heavens should be purified with these; but the heavenly things themselves with better sacrifices than these" (Heb. 9:23). I believe that in heaven Jesus Christ literally offered His blood; that He bore it to the Holy of Holies of which the tabernacle Holy of Holies is but a pattern. Now I know some people don't like to hear of the blood, and they consider such a literal interpretation to be crude. You will notice that the apostle Peter calls it the "precious blood of Christ." I believe that the blood of Christ will be at the throne of God to remind us throughout the endless ages of eternity that our salvation was purchased at a tremendous price. Christ shed His blood on the Cross and then He presented His blood for your sins and my sins. We have been redeemed by the precious blood of Christ.

PREPARATION OF THE PEOPLE

And when he hath made an end of reconciling the holy place, and the tabernacle of the congregation, and the altar, he shall bring the live goat:

And Aaron shall lay both his hands upon the head of the live goat, and confess over him all the iniquities of the children of Israel, and all their transgressions in all their sins, putting them upon the head of the goat, and shall send him away by the hand of a fit man into the wilderness:

And the goat shall bear upon him all their iniquities unto a land not inhabited: and he shall let go the goat in the wilderness [Lev. 16:20–22].

On this day the great high priest functioned alone. Aaron had sprinkled the blood of "the Lord's goat" on the mercy seat and now he places his bloody hands on the head of the live goat and confesses the sins of Israel. It must have been a sordid list of sins, but down the list he went. The laying on of hands denotes the fact that this goat is now identified as the sins of Israel.

Of Christ it is said, ". . . the Lord hath laid on him the iniquity of us all" (Isa. 53:6). "For he hath made him to be sin for us . . ." (2 Cor. 5:21) is reality. Ambrose said, "The thief knew that those wounds in the body of Christ were not the wounds of Christ, but of the thief."

Then Aaron put that goat into the hands of a man who had no personal interest in it, and Israelites were stationed at intervals to see that the job was done. The live goat finally disappeared into the wilderness, never to be seen or found again. The news that the goat was gone was relayed from station to station so that it was known a few minutes later in the temple.

Just as the news was passed from station to station, so the good news that Christ has taken away our sins has been passed from Matthew, Mark, Luke, and John to Paul the Apostle, then to the early church fathers, and finally to me and to you. Christ has put away our sins in a perfect and complete manner. The scapegoat illustrates several Scriptures in this connection: "As far as the east is from the west, so far hath he removed our transgressions from us" (Ps. 103:12). "Behold, for peace I had great bitterness: but thou hast in love to my soul delivered it from the pit of corruption: for thou hast cast all my sins behind thy back" (Isa. 38:17). "I have blotted out, as a thick cloud, thy transgressions, and, as a cloud, thy sins: return unto me; for I have redeemed thee" (Isa. 44:22). "In those days, and in that time, saith the LORD, the iniquity of Israel shall be sought for, and there shall be none; and the sins of Judah, and they shall not be found: for I will pardon them whom I reserve" (Jer. 50:20). "And they shall teach no more every man his neighbour, and every man his brother, saying, Know the LORD: for they shall all know me, from the least of them unto the greatest of them, saith the LORD: for I will remember their sin no more" (Jer. 31:34).

What does the great Day of Atonement mean to the Christian? It is a holy day for us too. When the high priest is there with his bloody hands on the head of the goat, I think of my Lord on the Cross. John pointed Him out, ". . . Behold the Lamb of God, which taketh away the sin of the world" (John 1:29).

". . . If we walk in the light, as he is in the light, we have fellowship one with another, and the blood of Jesus Christ his Son cleanseth us from all sin" (1 John 1:7). Dean Law has well said, "Faith transfers our sins; Christ removes them; God forgets them."

> **And Aaron shall come into the tabernacle of the congregation, and shall put off the linen garments, which he put on when he went into the holy place, and shall leave them there:**
>
> **And he shall wash his flesh with water in the holy place, and put on his garments, and come forth, and offer his burnt offering, and the burnt offering of the people, and make an atonement for himself, and for the people [Lev. 16:23–24].**

The ritual of the great Day of Atonement has now been completed. Without being irreverent, let me say that all that was left for Aaron to do was to wash up. This finds no counterpart in Christ. When His work was finished, He sat down at the right hand of God. Aaron did not *dare* enter the holy place for another year, but our Lord sits in the presence of the Father because there is no taint of sin upon Him now—even though He bore all sins upon the tree.

Verse 25 says that the fat of the sin offering is treated as a burnt offering. This protects the person of Christ from any implication of sin, even though He was made sin for us.

> **And he that let go the goat for the scapegoat shall wash his clothes, and bathe his flesh in water, and afterward come into the camp.**

> **And the bullock for the sin offering, and the goat for the sin offering, whose blood was brought in to make atonement in the holy place, shall one carry forth without the camp; and they shall burn in the fire their skins, and their flesh, and their dung.**

> **And he that burneth them shall wash his clothes, and bathe his flesh in water, and afterward he shall come into the camp [Lev. 16:26–28].**

The one who led the goat into the wilderness was contaminated by contact with the live goat and must wash his clothes and bathe himself. The carcasses of the bullock and goat were taken without the camp and burned, and the people who did that had to wash themselves. I tell you, God was impressing these people with the fact they were sinners, lost sinners. He is showing that He is holy and that sin separates from God. Friends, we were separated from God by sin, but Christ died for us. He is the One who took away our sins when He entered into the Holy Place with His own blood.

> **And this shall be a statute for ever unto you: that in the seventh month, on the tenth day of the month, ye shall**

afflict your souls, and do no work at all, whether it be one of your own country, or a stranger that sojourneth among you:

For on that day shall the priest make an atonement for you, to cleanse you, that ye may be clean from all your sins before the LORD.

It shall be a sabbath of rest unto you, and ye shall afflict your souls, by a statute for ever.

And the priest, whom he shall anoint, and whom he shall consecrate to minister in the priest's office in his father's stead, shall make the atonement, and shall put on the linen clothes, even the holy garments:

And he shall make an atonement for the holy sanctuary, and he shall make an atonement for the tabernacle of the congregation, and for the altar, and he shall make an atonement for the priests, and for all the people of the congregation.

And this shall be an everlasting statute unto you, to make an atonement for the children of Israel for all their sins once a year. And he did as the LORD commanded Moses [Lev. 16:29–34].

The Day of Atonement is the only day of mourning and fasting which God gave His people. On this day you don't say, "Happy Yom Kippur" or "Merry Yom Kippur" because that is not the way the day is celebrated. It was the day to afflict the soul because of sin. It was mourning for sin. This is the basis for fasting in the Old Testament.

This day was to be observed until the permanent and eternal sacrifice for sin came. It was fulfilled by Christ in His death.

"Man of Sorrows!" what a name
For the Son of God who came

Ruined sinners to reclaim!
Hallelujah! what a Saviour!

Bearing shame and scoffing rude,
In my place condemned He stood;
Sealed my pardon with His blood;
Hallelujah! what a Saviour!

Guilty, vile and helpless, we;
Spotless Lamb of God was He:
"Full atonement!" can it be?
Hallelujah! what a Saviour!

"Lifted up" was He to die,
"It is finished," was His cry;
Now in heav'n exalted high;
Hallelujah! what a Saviour!

When He comes, our glorious King,
All His ransomed home to bring,
Then anew this song we'll sing:
Hallelujah! what a Saviour!
                             —P. P. Bliss

CHAPTER 17

THEME: *One place of sacrifice; the offense of occult goat worship; the offering of sacrifice at the tabernacle; the obligation not to eat blood*

Leviticus is an exciting book as it is unfolding and opening up great basic and bedrock truths for the Christian today. Though these things were given to the nation Israel in a literal way, and though the reason for doing these things has passed away, yet all of this contains great spiritual lessons for us today. It answers many questions and gives new insights for the understanding and appreciation of the New Testament. I rejoice that many are coming to a personal relationship with Christ through the study of Leviticus.

Some people treat this chapter as an extension of the previous chapter. There is a sequence here, it is true, but the subject is different. Consideration is now given to the one place of sacrifice and the value of the blood.

This chapter had direct application to the wilderness march and the period that Israel was camped about the tabernacle. It has to do with ethical rather than ceremonial considerations. Clean domestic animals for food were to be slain at the tabernacle. Only verses 8 and 9 in this chapter have to do specifically with the ceremonial offering of a sacrifice to God.

After Israel was scattered throughout the land of Palestine, some of them lived a hundred or more miles from the tabernacle. It would not have been feasible or even possible for them to bring the animals they were to use for food and slay them at the tabernacle. In Deuteronomy God revised these instructions to them when they were ready to enter the land (Deut. 12:15–16, 20–25).

Why did God give such instructions? Israel was fresh out of Egypt where they had been surrounded by idolatry. They had worshiped the idols of Egypt, and there was always the danger of lapsing back to idolatry. They had worshiped the nature gods of Egypt. In verse 7 the word translated "devils" is actually *seirim* which means "hairy one" and refers to goats. The Egyptians worshiped Mendes, the goat god, and the Greeks worshiped the goat god as Pan—familiar to us from Greek literature and art depicted with tail, horns, and cloven feet. Medieval Christianity then identified this form as the devil. We get our word *panic* from this period of time when it described the terror that the Devil caused.

From this we see that Israel was forbidden to kill any animal in any place but the tabernacle in order to prevent them from making it an offering to Pan, the goat god.

Then, we learn that under no circumstance was the blood to be eaten. The reason is given specifically: it represents the life. There is a twofold reason behind this. (1) Life is sacred—even animals are not to be slain needlessly. (2) Blood speaks of the sacrifice of Christ. It was the means of expiation, the symbol of reconciliation, and the type of the one great vicarious, substitutionary sacrifice of Christ. Life is sacred and must be protected, but Christ must give His life so that the sinner can have life. Blood and life are synonymous. Man was never to eat blood. But he is to "drink the blood of Christ," which means to appropriate by faith in the shed blood of Christ the life of Christ which He gave up so that we might live. Let us love, praise, and talk about the blood. Too often, even in our churches, there is a soft-pedal placed on the topic of sin. My friend, it always follows that when there is a hesitation to mention sin, there is an equal playing down of the precious blood of Christ.

A famous preacher who came to Washington years ago was approached by a dowager who said, "Doctor, I do hope that you will not talk too much about the blood, as our former preacher did." His answer was enlightening, "Madam, I will not say too much about the blood." She interrupted, "I am so glad to hear that!" Then he added, "It is impossible to say too much about the blood!"

THE ONE PLACE OF SACRIFICE

And the Lord spake unto Moses, saying,

Speak unto Aaron, and unto his sons, and unto all the children of Israel, and say unto them; This is the thing which the LORD hath commanded, saying [Lev. 17:1–2].

These instructions were not for Moses and Aaron alone, but they were also for the sons of Aaron and for the entire nation of Israel. It is obvious that God is reaching now into the personal and private lives of the people. He not only made a difference between the clean and the unclean animals in chapter 11, but now He puts down the regulations by which they were to eat the clean animals. The lives of His people are to be different from the heathen round about them. They are told that again in the next chapter, as we shall see (Lev. 18:3).

What man soever there be of the house of Israel, that killeth an ox, or lamb, or goat, in the camp, or that killeth it out of the camp,

And bringeth it not unto the door of the tabernacle of the congregation, to offer an offering unto the LORD before the tabernacle of the LORD; blood shall be imputed unto that man; he hath shed blood; and that man shall be cut off from among his people:

To the end that the children of Israel may bring their sacrifices, which they offer in the open field, even that they may bring them unto the LORD, unto the door of the tabernacle of the congregation, unto the priest, and offer them for peace offerings unto the LORD.

And the priest shall sprinkle the blood upon the altar of the LORD at the door of the tabernacle of the congregation, and burn the fat for a sweet savour unto the LORD [Lev. 17:3–6].

This is another of those strange laws and it does not concern the ceremonial offering of sacrifices. When you look at it carefully, you will note that these animals were for food for God's people. In other words,

God is demanding that they bring Him to the dinner table! By this token, the heathen gods were shut out.

Why was God so strict about this? If they were going to have a lamb for dinner, they had to bring it to the door of the tabernacle to slay it. Maybe some of them didn't want their neighbors to know they were having company. Maybe some of them forgot to invite their mother-in-law for dinner. All this made no difference. They must slay the animal at the tabernacle. This was done because of their background. You see, among the heathen the meat was offered to an idol before it was eaten. God was putting up a roadblock to hinder His people from taking the long road to idolatry, spiritual darkness, and judgment.

When they lived down in Egypt, even though they were in slavery, they were idolaters just like the Egyptians. God did not redeem them because they were superior. God redeemed them because He had heard their cry and because He had made a promise to Abraham, Isaac, and Jacob. When God makes a covenant, He keeps it. How do I know they were idolaters in Egypt? Because Scripture says they were. "In the day that I lifted up mine hand unto them, to bring them forth of the land of Egypt into a land that I had espied for them, flowing with milk and honey, which is the glory of all lands: Then said I unto them, Cast ye away every man the abominations of his eyes, and defile not yourselves with the idols of Egypt: I am the LORD your God. But they rebelled against me, and would not hearken unto me: they did not every man cast away the abominations of their eyes, neither did they forsake the idols of Egypt: then I said, I will pour out my fury upon them, to accomplish my anger against them in the midst of the land of Egypt" (Ezek. 20:6–8). God is trying to break them from that sordid background in the land of Egypt. They had worshiped animals, and the shedding of blood and the offering of the meat were used in idolatry.

One needs to understand this background to get the significance of Paul's injunctions to the Corinthians in 1 Corinthians 8:1–13 and 10:1–33. The Corinthians were idolatrous and they brought their animal and offered it to their idols. They left their animal there; the meat was taken into the temple and sold in the meat market there. The best filet mignon of that day would have been bought at the heathen temple; it was the local supermarket. By the time of the New Testament, the godly Israelite had been so schooled that he refused to buy this meat that had been offered to idols. The converted Gentiles didn't have any qualms about eating the meat that had been offered to idols, realizing that the idol was nothing. But the Jewish Christian didn't like to eat with the gentile Christian because of this difference over meat offered to idols. This chapter in Leviticus, you see, gives the background for the passage to the Corinthians.

It is interesting to note that when the great Council of Jerusalem handed down the decision, James spoke for the group and said, "Wherefore my sentence is, that we trouble not them, which from among the Gentiles are turned to God: but that we write unto them, that they abstain from pollutions of idols, and from fornication, and from things strangled, and from blood" (Acts 15:19–20). God was teaching the gentile believers that life is sacred.

May I mention here that the slaughter of animals for food is still associated with heathen worship among the Hindus and in Persia.

Actually, the children of Israel had very little meat to eat in the wilderness. I think the incident concerning the quail indicated that. They complained because they didn't have any meat to eat and cried, ". . . Who shall give us flesh to eat?" (Num. 11:4). This was true of all nations of antiquity, and even today nations in the East are short on meat. Some are actually vegetarian in their diets.

A clean animal for food for the table was to be killed at the door of the tabernacle. The blood would be poured out there. The blood was placed upon the altar, and the fat was offered as a sweet savour. The sacrifice was a peace offering. The remainder of the animal was returned to the owner, and he could prepare it for his table. You can see why the Jewish believers resented the Gentiles eating meat bought at a heathen temple.

THE OFFENSE OF OCCULT GOAT WORSHIP

And they shall no more offer their sacrifices unto devils, after whom they have gone a-whoring. This shall be a

**statute for ever unto them throughout their generations
[Lev. 17:7].**

I have already mentioned that the word *devils* in this verse is literally
"hairy ones," or goats. The same word is used in 2 Chronicles 11:15:
"And he ordained him priests for the high places, and for the devils
[literally, goats], and for the calves which he had made." That is how
Jeroboam, the son of Nebat, made Israel to sin.

This refers to nature worship, degrading and licentious, associated with the god Pan. God is saying to His people, "Don't you do
that! You bring that animal to the door of the tabernacle." This is why
there was the severe penalty as stated in the fourth verse. The details
had to be changed when they entered into the land, but the principle
that is taught here is eternal.

This is very, very important for us to see today. They lived under
the danger of returning to idolatry and to gross immorality, and right
now we are experiencing a return to this matter of nature worship. My
friend, all this business today of going back to primitive living is a
return to the same sort of thing. God wanted to protect them and
wants to protect us from idolatry and immorality.

THE OFFERING OF SACRIFICE
AT THE TABERNACLE

**And thou shalt say unto them, Whatsoever man there be
of the house of Israel, or of the strangers which sojourn
among you, that offereth a burnt offering or sacrifice,**

**And bringeth it not unto the door of the tabernacle of the
congregation, to offer it unto the LORD; even that man
shall be cut off from among his people [Lev. 17:8–9].**

God is specific about bringing an animal for their own food or bringing it for an offering. God did not let them present an animal as an

offering and then take it home to eat. Now, in these two verses, He is talking about bringing an animal for a burnt offering. When the animal was brought as an offering, they had to make the offering according to the law of the burnt offering. There was only one place for sacrifice. The Lord repeated this again and again in order to deter Israel from idolatry.

It was applicable to the strangers and foreigners who had established residence in Israel. There was always the danger of the influence from the presence of the heathen in their midst. The tendency was to resort to the ways of the heathen rather than to win them over to the Lord.

We are told today, "Wherefore, my dearly beloved, flee from idolatry" (1 Cor. 10:14). And again, "Be ye not unequally yoked together with unbelievers: for what fellowship hath righteousness with unrighteousness? and what communion hath light with darkness? And what concord hath Christ with Belial? . . . Wherefore come out from among them, and be ye separate, saith the Lord, and touch not the unclean thing; and I will receive you" (2 Cor. 6:14–17).

This is a great principle which is carried over to the church. There is a danger of association with the unbeliever in religion, politics, marriage, business, or social life. God has placed a warning about this in His Word.

THE OBLIGATION NOT TO EAT BLOOD

And whatsoever man there be of the house of Israel, or of the strangers that sojourn among you, that eateth any manner of blood; I will even set my face against that soul that eateth blood, and will cut him off from among his people.

For the life of the flesh is in the blood: and I have given it to you upon the altar to make an atonement for your souls: for it is the blood that maketh an atonement for the soul [Lev. 17:10–11].

I consider verse 11 one of the key verses of this book. The life is in the blood. This is restated in verse 14. This is the basis of all sacrifice.

> **Therefore I said unto the children of Israel, No soul of you shall eat blood, neither shall any stranger that sojourneth among you eat blood.**
>
> **And whatsoever man there be of the children of Israel, or of the strangers that sojourn among you, which hunteth and catcheth any beast or fowl that may be eaten; he shall even pour out the blood thereof, and cover it with dust.**
>
> **For it is the life of all flesh; the blood of it is for the life thereof: therefore I said unto the children of Israel, Ye shall eat the blood of no manner of flesh: for the life of all flesh is the blood thereof: whosoever eateth it shall be cut off [Lev. 17:12–14].**

Jesus Christ said something very interesting. "Whoso eateth my flesh, and drinketh my blood, hath eternal life; and I will raise him up at the last day. For my flesh is meat indeed, and my blood is drink indeed. He that eateth my flesh, and drinketh my blood, dwelleth in me, and I in him" (John 6:54–56). Because the life of the flesh is in the blood, Jesus is saying that we are to accept His shed blood for our sins by faith and then we receive life. Jesus shed His blood and gave His life. The life is in the blood.

This is a great, eternal truth. This explains why Abel's sacrifice was more excellent than Cain's. It is the blood that maketh an atonement for the soul. The blood of Christ is the only thing that can wash away sin. There is nothing offensive about the blood; the offense is in our sin.

> What can wash away my sin?
> Nothing but the blood of Jesus;
> What can make me whole again?

Nothing but the blood of Jesus.
Oh! precious is the flow
That makes me white as snow;
No other fount I know,
Nothing but the blood of Jesus.

CHAPTER 18

THEME: Immorality condemned, amplification of the seventh commandment—preamble to social prohibitions; sexual relations with relatives forbidden; sundry sexual sins prohibited; offspring forbidden to be offered to Molech; perversion of sex prohibited; nations in Palestine cast out for committing these sins

Up to this point the laws concerning ceremonial cleansing have been given. The rules regulated the ritual of religion. In chapters 18, 19, and 20, we find a special section which applies the Ten Commandments to life situations. God is now dealing with the moral aspects of the lives of His people. Friends, we are getting right down to the nitty-gritty.

This section opens with a preamble in 18:1–5 and closes with a formal postscript at the close of chapter 20. These are very important because they give the reason for the restrictions and regulations of the social life of His people.

We are living in a day when the moral foundations have been broken up and removed. "Who makes the rules, and what is right and wrong?" asks the sneering skeptic. This preamble and postscript give us a twofold explanation:

(1) Three times in the preamble, verses 2, 4, and 5, the Word says, "I am the LORD." God makes the rules! Breaking the Ten Commandments is wrong because God says it is wrong. (2) The postscript gives the second reason. "And ye shall be holy unto me: for I the LORD am holy, and have severed you from other people, that ye should be mine" (Lev. 20:26). God demands that His people be holy. Purity in all life's situations is the command of God.

This chapter deals with the seventh commandment primarily. It spells out in detail what is meant by adultery. Sexual sins are the subject. These are the sins which mark a decadent society and the decline and fall of empires.

PREAMBLE TO SOCIAL PROHIBITIONS

And the LORD spake unto Moses, saying,

Speak unto the children of Israel, and say unto them, I am the LORD your God.

After the doings of the land of Egypt, wherein ye dwelt, shall ye not do: and after the doings of the land of Canaan, whither I bring you, shall ye not do; neither shall ye walk in their ordinances.

Ye shall do my judgments, and keep mine ordinances, to walk therein: I am the LORD your God.

Ye shall therefore keep my statutes, and my judgments: which if a man do, he shall live in them: I am the LORD [Lev. 18:1-5].

They have just come out of Egypt, and there they had done all these things which are forbidden. The disgusting sins which will be mentioned were a way of life for the Egyptians. God has to separate His people from the influence of that sinful environment. They were going to the land of Canaan, a land flowing with milk and honey. But that isn't all that was in Canaan—the Canaanites were there, and they also were immoral. God saw that the children of Israel were caught, as we would say, between the devil and the deep blue sea, or between a rock and a hard place. The Egyptians were behind them, the Canaanites were ahead of them, and both of them were grossly immoral.

We are living in a day when they talk about a sexual revolution. I wonder whether people have read the eighteenth chapter of Leviticus. May I say to you, there is nothing new about sexual perversion at all. It is the same old immorality that they had in Egypt and in Canaan.

God says, "I am the LORD your God," and "I am the LORD." Who makes the rules? God makes the rules. Maybe someone says, "But I don't want to follow them." Well, that is up to you, but God still makes the rules! Breaking the Ten Commandments is wrong because God says it is wrong. That ought to be enough to satisfy the heart of the child of God. The skeptic would not be satisfied with any argument since he makes his own rules, and he is his own god.

By the way, if you can create a whole universe—and you will need a whole planetary system with a sun and a moon and a few stars—then you can make your own ten commandments. But as long as you are living in God's world, breathing His air, using His sunshine, drinking His water, walking on His earth, and not even paying rent for it, you had better obey His commands. He tells us that if we break His commandments, we will pay for it. And, my friend, you will pay! You may not be arrested by the local police, but you will stand before Him some day.

The things that God said were immoral are still immoral today. Listen to the New Testament: "Not in the lust of concupisence, even as the Gentiles which know not God: That no man go beyond and defraud his brother in any matter: because that the Lord is the avenger of all such, as we also have forewarned you and testified. For God hath not called us unto uncleanness, but unto holiness" (1 Thess. 4:5–7). "This I say therefore, and testify in the Lord, that ye henceforth walk not as other Gentiles walk, in the vanity of their mind, having the understanding darkened, being alienated from the life of God through the ignorance that is in them, because of the blindness of their heart: who being past feeling have given themselves over into lasciviousness, to work all uncleanness with greediness" (Eph. 4:17–19). "But now I have written unto you not to keep company, if any man that is called a brother be a fornicator, or covetous, or an idolater, or a railer, or a drunkard, or an extortioner; with such an one no not to eat" (1 Cor. 5:11). "Whereby are given unto us exceeding great and precious promises: that by these ye might be partakers of the divine nature, having escaped the corruption that is in the world through lust" (2 Pet. 1:4).

These passages from the Epistles of the New Testament are speaking to you and to me. The child of God in any age is called to holy living. "Know ye not that ye are the temple of God, and that the Spirit of God dwelleth in you? If any man defile the temple of God, him shall God destroy; for the temple of God is holy, which temple ye are" (1 Cor. 3:16–17). "According as he hath chosen us in him before the foundation of the world, that we should be holy and without blame before him in love" (Eph. 1:4). "Because it is written, Be ye holy; for I am holy" (1 Pet. 1:16). God is calling us to holiness. We need to emphasize holiness. God asks us to be holy.

There is another truth that I do not want you to miss, friends. Many folk say that if you are going to reach the crowds, you've got to go down and live with them. You've got to be like they are. This has been tried, both by individuals and by groups. And do you know what? They don't reach the crowd; they become a part of the crowd. May I say to you, God has called us to holiness. Folk who have really reached men for Christ have been those whose *lives* commended the gospel they preached. For example, England was a pretty wicked place during the eighteenth century, and they called the followers of John Wesley, "holy people." In fact, they gave them the name "Methodists" because their methods were different from the methods of the world.

God says, "I am Jehovah." Someone may say, "Well, I'm not a Christian, and I'm just not interested." May I say to you that God is declaring His sovereignty. God created this universe and He is the One who is running it. And He says, "I am your God." He is a reconciled God. He knows our frame and yet He loves us. Friend, if you are reconciled to God, you will want to please Him. The child of God can be filled with the Holy Spirit so that he will not commit these sins of the flesh, but will produce the fruit of the Spirit.

SEXUAL RELATIONS WITH RELATIVES FORBIDDEN

> None of you shall approach to any that is near of kin to him, to uncover their nakedness: I am the LORD [Lev. 18:6].

The blanket statement is made that no person is to have sexual relations with a near relative. This entire section amplifies the seventh commandment. Here it refers to anyone who has the same blood relationship as the other person. Now it goes on. God is specific. And the reason He gives is, "I am the LORD."

> The nakedness of thy father, or the nakedness of thy mother, shalt thou not uncover: she is thy mother; thou shalt not uncover her nakedness.

> The nakedness of thy father's wife shalt thou not uncover: it is thy father's nakedness [Lev. 18:7–8].

This warns against disgusting incest. Yet this sin was in the Corinthian church. Paul condemned it with great feeling. "It is reported commonly that there is fornication among you, and such fornication as is not so much as named among the Gentiles, that one should have his father's wife" (1 Cor. 5:1).

These are things that are talked about today, aren't they? Well, God talks about them, too. Don't tell me things are different today. God has spelled out exactly what is sin. Nobody can make a mistake about this, friends.

> The nakedness of thy sister, the daughter of thy father, or daughter of thy mother, whether she be born at home, or born abroad, even their nakedness thou shalt not uncover.

> The nakedness of thy son's daughter, or of thy daughter's daughter, even their nakedness thou shalt not uncover: for theirs is thine own nakedness.

> The nakedness of thy father's wife's daughter, begotten of thy father, she is thy sister, thou shalt not uncover her nakedness.

> Thou shalt not uncover the nakedness of thy father's sister: she is thy father's near kinswoman.

> Thou shalt not uncover the nakedness of thy mother's sister: for she is thy mother's near kinswoman.

> Thou shalt not uncover the nakedness of thy father's brother, thou shalt not approach to his wife: she is thine aunt.

> **Thou shalt not uncover the nakedness of thy daughter-in-law: she is thy son's wife: thou shalt not uncover her nakedness [Lev. 18:9–15].**

The different human relationships which are established by blood or marriage are dealt with specifically in this section. Relatives are thrown together in a domestic situation in which adultery could be practiced. God put up these barriers to prevent this.

Egypt practiced these sins, especially those mentioned in verse 9. The Pharaohs and the Ptolemies practiced intermarriage of brother and sister.

In the beginning, there was no law against this. Cain and Seth had to marry their own sisters. Abraham married his half sister. However the Law now halts this practice.

> **Thou shalt not uncover the nakedness of thy brother's wife: it is thy brother's nakedness [Lev. 18:16].**

There is an exception to this verse and that is in the law of the kinsman-redeemer as stated in Deuteronomy 25:5–10.

SUNDRY SEXUAL SINS PROHIBITED

> **Thou shalt not uncover the nakedness of a woman and her daughter, neither shalt thou take her son's daughter, or her daughter's daughter, to uncover her nakedness; for they are her near kinswomen: it is wickedness.**
>
> **Neither shalt thou take a wife to her sister, to vex her, to uncover her nakedness, beside the other in her life time [Lev. 18:17–18].**

This relationship is not by blood, but by marriage. Because of the close relationship of the wife to a daughter or son, any marriage is forbidden. Evidently both of these verses have reference to having two wives at the same time. It is labeled incest here, instead of bigamy. Notice the Berkeley Version on these two verses: "Do not expose the nakedness of both a woman and her daughter; neither take her son's daughter or her daughter's daughter to expose her; they are blood relatives. It is incest. While your wife is still living do not take her sister for a rival to expose her nakedness" (Lev. 18:17–18).

This was the problem poor Jacob faced in having two sisters as wives—Leah and Rachel. The story of this family was certainly not a happy one. Remember, however, that Jacob lived before the Ten Commandments had been given.

Also thou shalt not approach unto a woman to uncover her nakedness, as long as she is put apart for her uncleanness [Lev. 18:19].

Lawful marital relations of a husband and wife were forbidden at certain times. The sensual mind must be made subject to the Law of God.

Moreover thou shalt not lie carnally with thy neighbour's wife, to defile thyself with her [Lev. 18:20].

Believe me, God is throwing up these bulwarks to protect the home from the licentious practices of the heathen round about them. The family on earth was to mirror the family in heaven (Eph. 3:15). Purity of living was to be the badge of God's family. There was a holy place in the tabernacle for *worship;* the home was a holy place in the nation for *living.* The New Testament also has a great deal about this. It would be well to read 1 Corinthians 7 in this connection.

OFFSPRING FORBIDDEN
TO BE OFFERED TO MOLECH

And thou shalt not let any of thy seed pass through the fire to Molech, neither shalt thou profane the name of thy God: I am the LORD [Lev. 18:21].

"Thy seed" means their children. This verse may seem to be out of place in this chapter, but the pagan worship of Molech was closely related with sex. The image of old Molech was heated red hot, and the bodies of children were placed in its arms. It is hard to imagine the horror of this. There are those who believe that such a thing could never have happened. However, the Scriptures make other references to this same practice. ". . . and the Sepharvites burnt their children in fire to Adrammelech and Anammelech, the gods of Sepharvaim" (2 Kings 17:31). "And they have built the high places of Tophet, which is in the valley of the son of Hinnom, to burn their sons and their daughters in the fire; which I commanded them not, neither came it into my heart" (Jer. 7:31). This terrible practice profanes the holy name of God (Lev. 20:3). The unnatural brutality of this pagan rite was a deep profaning of the name of the true God. God's love of children is evident in Scripture from Genesis to Revelation. The Lord Jesus said, "Let them come to Me."

PERVERSION OF SEX PROHIBITED

Thou shalt not lie with mankind, as with womankind: it is abomination [Lev. 18:22].

It is hard to believe that right here in downtown Los Angeles, a church put on a dance for sexual perverts. I am told they had over 700 people at that dance. It was so disgusting that a hard-boiled newspaper writer went down to write it up, but walked out. Yet a "church" engaged in that. My friend, God condemns it! In the Old Testament He condemns it; in the New Testament He condemns it. "Wherefore God also gave them up to uncleanness through the lusts of their own hearts, to dishonour their own bodies between themselves: Who changed the truth of God into a lie, and worshipped and served the creature more than the Creator, who is blessed for ever. Amen. For this cause God gave them up unto vile affections: for even their women did change the natural use into that which is against nature: And likewise also the men, leaving the natural use of the woman, burned in their lust one toward another; men with men working that which is unseemly, and receiving in themselves that recompence of their error which was meet. And even as they did not like to retain God in their knowledge, God gave them over to a reprobate mind, to do those things which are not convenient" (Rom. 1:24–28).

The depravity that is mentioned here is common today. The United States is like Sodom and Gomorrah. It makes me weep to see the way my country is going. I love this country. It's the land of my birth. I hate to see these dirty, filthy, immoral people bringing us into judgment. Believe me, friends, the judgment of God is already upon us today. We can't have peace abroad and we can't have peace at home, Why not? "There is no peace, saith the LORD, unto the wicked" (Isa. 48:22).

Neither shalt thou lie with any beast to defile thyself therewith: neither shall any woman stand before a beast to lie down thereto: it is confusion [Lev. 18:23].

This is indeed unspeakable. This was practiced in the fertility cults and nature worship. Licentiousness is always connected with idolatry in the most debased fashion. And if you think this is not being practiced today, then you should talk to the police department in a city like Los Angeles. They can tell you.

NATIONS IN PALESTINE CAST OUT
FOR COMMITTING THESE SINS

Defile not ye yourselves in any of these things: for in all these the nations are defiled which I cast out before you:

And the land is defiled: therefore I do visit the iniquity thereof upon it, and the land itself vomiteth out her inhabitants [Lev. 18:24–25].

The nations in Palestine were cast out because they committed these abominable and atrocious sins. That is the reason they were put off the land. A lot of soft-hearted and soft-headed preachers today weep because God put out the Canaanites. Here is the reason God put them out. God couldn't tolerate what was taking place. The land of the Canaanites was eaten up with venereal disease. Why do you suppose God told them not to take even a wedge of gold or to touch a garment in the city of Jericho? They were guilty of the vilest sins imaginable. Don't you think that God put them out for a good reason? After all, if the tenant doesn't pay rent, he can be put out. God happened to own that land.

My friend, that is the way you and I occupy this earth down here. Our "three score years and ten" is just a lease. The land is God's. It is His business and it would be well for us to make His business our business. His business is the one that will prevail.

Ye shall therefore keep my statutes and my judgments, and shall not commit any of these abominations; neither any of your own nation, nor any stranger that sojourneth among you:

(For all these abominations have the men of the land done, which were before you, and the land is defiled;)

That the land spue not you out also, when ye defile it, as it spued out the nations that were before you.

For whosoever shall commit any of these abominations, even the souls that commit them shall be cut off from among their people.

Therefore shall ye keep mine ordinance, that ye commit not any one of these abominable customs, which were committed before you, and that ye defile not yourselves therein: I am the LORD your God [Lev. 18:26–30].

God gives a double warning to His people that if they pursue a pattern similar to those who preceded them in the land, the same judgment, if not worse, would befall them. God's land must be holy. God's ultimate goal is that righteousness will cover the earth.

CHAPTER 19

THEME: Man's relationship to God; man's relationship to the poor; man's relationship to his neighbour; man's relationships in different life situations

We are in that section of the book where the Ten Commandments are explained in terms of the social life of the nation. I can't think of anything more practical than this particular section. God's law is to tell us this one thing: ". . . Ye shall be holy: for I the Lord your God am holy" (Lev. 19:2). This was fundamental and basic to all facets of the life of Israel. It explained everything which God commanded or demanded. It entered into the web and woof of their daily routine. Holiness in daily life with all of its relationships was paramount in the everyday living of God's people. That is something that needs to be reemphasized today, by the way. This is not just theory. God intended it to be brought right into our lives.

The Law cannot produce the holiness which it demands. It demanded, but it did not supply. It revealed the righteousness of the Law, but the high level which it demanded could not be attained by human effort. "Now we know that what things soever the law saith, it saith to them who are under the law: that every mouth may be stopped, and all the world may become guilty before God. Therefore by the deeds of the law there shall no flesh be justified in his sight: for by the law is the knowledge of sin" (Rom. 3:19–20).

How wonderful it is that God has given us His Holy Spirit to indwell us. This is the dynamic that is needed for Christian living.

The reason given in this chapter, "I am the Lord your God" or "I am the Lord" occurs sixteen times in this chapter. God draws the line between right and wrong. He alone makes the sharp distinction between the holy and unholy. No other reason needs to be given.

MAN'S RELATIONSHIP TO GOD

And the LORD spake unto Moses, saying,

Speak unto all the congregation of the children of Israel, and say unto them, Ye shall be holy: for I the LORD your God am holy [Lev. 19:1-2].

God gives these instructions to Moses the lawgiver, and they amplify a portion of the Ten Commandments. God exacts holy conduct on the basis that He is holy. It is well to note that God still enjoins the same conduct today. "Whether therefore ye eat, or drink, or whatsoever ye do, do all to the glory of God" (1 Cor. 10:31). "Therefore if any man be in Christ, he is a new creature: old things are passed away; behold, all things are become new" (2 Cor. 5:17). "Wherefore gird up the loins of your mind, be sober, and hope to the end for the grace that is to be brought unto you at the revelation of Jesus Christ; as obedient children, not fashioning yourselves according to the former lusts in your ignorance: but as he which hath called you is holy, so be ye holy in all manner of conversation; because it is written, Be ye holy; for I am holy" (1 Pet. 1:13-16).

The major difference between the conduct required under law and under grace is that today the dynamic is supplied to the believer in the person of the Holy Spirit. We are joined to the living Christ. Old things have passed away. We are no longer joined to Adam, and we are no longer joined to a legal system. We are joined to Christ and we are to seek to please Him. You see, under the Law they tried to keep the commandments by their own effort. They were to learn that the flesh will always fail. In contrast to this, we have the Spirit of God in us. "For what the law could not do, in that it was weak through the flesh, God sending his own Son in the likeness of sinful flesh, and for sin, condemned sin in the flesh: that the righteousness of the law might be fulfilled in us, who walk not after the flesh, but after the Spirit" (Rom. 8:3-4). "But the fruit of the Spirit is love, joy, peace, longsuffering, gentleness, goodness, faith, meekness, temperance: against

such there is no law" (Gal. 5:22–23). The Law never went as far as
this. The Son of God wants to bring us up to a high plane.

Now, in emphasizing certain of the commandments they were to
keep, God will emphasize those particular areas in which they were
weak. The history of Israel will show us that God understood their
weak points. They were instructed about the Sabbath, the avoidance
of idolatry, the bringing of proper offerings to God. These are areas in
which they later broke down. God is asking them to be holy in their
daily life.

**Ye shall fear every man his mother, and his father, and
keep my sabbaths: I am the Lord your God [Lev. 19:3].**

One might think it is strange that God should begin with the commandment to honor father and mother. But it is not so strange when
we consider that the parent stands in the place of God for the child and
that the child learns to obey God by first obeying the parent. When
you are going to get down to the nitty-gritty, you must begin at home.

Then He adds, "And keep my sabbaths." God demanded one-
seventh of man's time as well as one-tenth of his possessions.

These two commandments mentioned first encompass the two
major divisions of the Ten Commandments. There is duty to man and
duty to God. The Lord Jesus Christ summed it all up as love to God
and love to man. He said this is the sum total of the law (Matt. 22:36–
40).

The Sabbath law does not rest upon a moral basis but was an arbi-
trary command of God given to Israel. Israel, in apostasy and decline,
sinned at this point. They refused to observe the sabbaths. "Saying,
When will the new moon be gone, that we may sell corn? and the
sabbath, that we may set forth wheat, making the ephah small, and
the shekel great, and falsifying the balances by deceit?" (Amos 8:5).
This was God's charge and case against the nation.

**Turn ye not unto idols, nor make to yourselves molten
gods: I am the Lord your God [Lev. 19:4].**

This covers the first two commandments. The thought here is not even to cast a glance at idolatry. Heathen worship appealed to the eye with its pomp and ceremony. It still does. Look at the pageantry and meaningless rituals that you see in religion today. It is "eye service." They were not to look on idols and they were not to make idols. God ridicules the idols because they are nothing and can do nothing.

> **And if ye offer a sacrifice of peace offerings unto the Lord, ye shall offer it at your own will.**
>
> **It shall be eaten the same day ye offer it, and on the morrow: and if aught remain until the third day, it shall be burnt in the fire.**
>
> **And if it be eaten at all on the third day, it is abominable: it shall not be accepted.**
>
> **Therefore every one that eateth it shall bear his iniquity, because he hath profaned the hallowed thing of the Lord: and that soul shall be cut off from among his people [Lev. 19:5–8].**

There is nothing new added here. However, we should point out again that the peace offering was to be made voluntarily. Even though it was a voluntary offering, the offerer was not relieved from following scrupulously the rules that were prescribed. Any deviation from the prescribed order penalized the man as an example to the people.

I find today that there are those in Christian service who seem to think they can take special liberties that no one else can take. Or some people think that because they have given a large contribution to the church they should have special privileges and special attention. Notice that the peace offering was given voluntarily, but the detail had to be followed through meticulously. We must all come to God on God's terms. Any deviation from the prescribed order penalized the man as an example to the people. This was a positive law, not a moral law. Because of that, there was the more danger of failure. How many people today make a pledge to the church and then feel that they don't need to go through with it if they don't wish to. God says, "If you are going to do it voluntarily, then do it right."

I had to go out to a television station to make a tape to be aired locally. They were taping a very popular program and so I stayed to watch. I was so impressed by the dedication of the people who were putting it on that I stayed a long time to watch and someone might ask me why I did that. Well, I've been among Christians so long that it did me good to get among people who were dedicated. Of course I understand why they are dedicated—they are dedicated to greed. They were being paid a handsome sum to do that show, but I'll tell you, they gave it everything they had.

Too many Christians excuse what they are doing by saying it is just volunteer work. God may say, "If you are going to do it, then do it right when you come to Me." Don't volunteer to do God's work unless you are going to give it everything you have. I'm of the opinion there will be a lot of Christians judged someday because of their laziness. Some folk glory in the fact they took a job. "Look, I taught a Sunday school class." My friend, how many times were you late? How many times did you fail to prepare the lesson? I tell you, the crowd in the television show knew their parts. But I see Sunday school teachers flipping through the quarterly, trying to find something to say. I think God is going to judge us on that someday. He tells us not to come to Him with a voluntary offering unless we come the right way.

MAN'S RELATIONSHIP TO THE POOR

And when ye reap the harvest of your land, thou shalt not wholly reap the corners of thy field, neither shalt thou gather the gleanings of thy harvest.

And thou shalt not glean thy vineyard, neither shalt thou gather every grape of thy vineyard; thou shalt leave them for the poor and stranger: I am the LORD your God [Lev. 19:9–10].

This was God's marvelous provision for the poor. God did not put anyone on charity. He never let anyone sit down and do nothing and receive a welfare check. The poor were taken care of by being given the opportunity to work. This was a marvelous balance between heartless capitalism and godless socialism. Whatever a farmer did not reap his first time around must be left for the poor. The ancient method of harvesting by hand left 10 percent to 20 percent of the grain in the field. The same law applied to their vineyards. I was at a meeting in Turlock, California, and a man told me to go out to the vineyard and help myself to the grapes because he knew how I loved grapes. It was after the harvest and the pickers were all gone. I could have filled a truck with grapes if I had had one there. That night at the meeting I told the folk that I had been out gleaning. That is the way God took care of His people. His method of dealing with poverty enabled both rich and poor to acknowledge the good hand of God.

MAN'S RELATIONSHIP TO HIS NEIGHBOR

Ye shall not steal, neither deal falsely, neither lie one to another.

And ye shall not swear by my name falsely, neither shalt thou profane the name of thy God: I am the LORD [Lev. 19:11–12].

This restates the eighth and ninth commandments. "Thou shalt not steal. Thou shalt not bear false witness against thy neighbour" (Exod. 20:15–16). Stealing, defrauding, lying, and perjury are all included here. To deal falsely is a form of stealing according to God's definition.

The third commandment is included in verse 12. God's name is holy. In business God's man is to demonstrate the holiness of God's name by his honest and true business dealings.

Thou shalt not defraud thy neighbour, neither rob him: the wages of him that is hired shall not abide with thee all night until the morning [Lev. 19:13].

We are to pay any man working for us. May I say to you, I think God would be on the side of labor. My dad was a working man and I remember him in overalls more than any other way. He built cotton gins in Texas and many times, I found out, he was beaten financially. Listen to James: "Go to now, ye rich men, weep and howl for your miseries that shall come upon you. Your riches are corrupted, and your garments are moth-eaten" (James 5:1–2). Verse 6 of the same chapter goes on to say, "Ye have condemned and killed the just; and he doth not resist you." Godless labor is a terrible thing and so is godless capitalism. Right now I think we are in real danger from the latter.

> **Thou shalt not curse the deaf, nor put a stumblingblock before the blind, but shalt fear thy God: I am the Lord [Lev. 19:14].**

A blind man told me how he was cheated by a salesman who came to him. May I say to you, these terrible things are still done today. God put a double emphasis on His name in consideration of the deaf and blind. It is God's concern for the weak, helpless, and infirm, and it is His rebuke against the hardheartedness of man.

> **Ye shall do no unrighteousness in judgment: thou shalt not respect the person of the poor, nor honour the person of the mighty: but in righteousness shalt thou judge thy neighbour [Lev. 19:15].**

Here is a word for the judge sitting on the bench, and how our judges need this word today! The judge on the bench is to understand that he is to judge as God judges. I wish some of them would remember that they are in that position, not because some politician put them there, but because they represent Almighty God. And they are to judge impartially.

Shakespeare wrote in *King Henry VIII*: "Heaven is above all yet; there sits a judge that no king can corrupt." Socrates said, "Four things belong to a judge, to hear courteously, to answer wisely, to consider soberly, and to decide impartially."

> Thou shalt not go up and down as a talebearer among
> thy people: neither shalt thou stand against the blood of
> thy neighbour: I am the LORD.
>
> Thou shalt not hate thy brother in thine heart: thou shalt
> in any wise rebuke thy neighbour, and not suffer sin
> upon him.
>
> Thou shalt not avenge, nor bear any grudge against the
> children of thy people, but thou shalt love thy neighbour
> as thyself: I am the LORD [Lev. 19:16–18].

Talebearing is slander. It is best to remain silent if to tell the truth will
ruin a neighbor.

Sir Walter Scott wrote, "Low breathed talkers, minion lispers cut-
ting honest throats by whispers." Someone else has said, "You cannot
believe everything you hear, but you can repeat it." James has a great
deal to say about this, and I wrote a little booklet on his epistle called
Tongues on Fire. Do you know what tongues on fire is? It is the little
tongue that is in your mouth. It is an awful thing. It is the most dangerous thing in the world, more dangerous than an atom bomb.

"Stand against the blood" means to murder. Hatred is not put on a
par with murder, but it is forbidden. Our Lord linked them together
and said that if you hate, you are a murderer (Matt. 5:21–22).

The answer to all these negative prohibitions is found in the positive, "But thou shalt love thy neighbour as thyself." Paul summed up
all this for the Christian: "Brethren, if a man be overtaken in a fault,
ye which are spiritual, restore such an one in the spirit of meekness;
considering thyself, lest thou also be tempted" (Gal. 6:1).

MAN'S RELATIONSHIPS
IN DIFFERENT LIFE SITUATIONS

> Ye shall keep my statutes. Thou shalt not let thy cattle
> gender with a diverse kind: thou shalt not sow thy field
> with mingled seed: neither shall a garment mingled of
> linen and woollen come upon thee [Lev. 19:19].

Do you know what happens when you wash such a garment? God is teaching them great spiritual truths with symbols and ceremonies. They were not to have hybrid animals and plants. This was to teach them that there is to be no mingling of truth and error. This is brought out by our Lord's parable of the wheat and the tares (Matt. 13). Paul says, "Ye cannot drink the cup of the Lord, and the cup of devils: Ye cannot be partakers of the Lord's table, and of the table of devils" (1 Cor. 10:21). Christ said, ". . . Ye cannot serve God and mammon" (Luke 16:13).

And whosoever lieth carnally with a woman, that is a bondmaid, betrothed to an husband, and not at all redeemed, nor freedom given her; she shall be scourged; they shall not be put to death, because she was not free.

And he shall bring his trespass offering unto the LORD, unto the door of the tabernacle of the congregation, even a ram for a trespass offering.

And the priest shall make an atonement for him with the ram of the trespass offering before the LORD for his sin which he hath done: and the sin which he hath done shall be forgiven him [Lev. 19:20-22].

This goes back to the seventh commandment. This protects the bondwoman. This raises the natural question, "Is God lending approval to slavery?" No. God is recognizing the sinful situation caused by the hard hearts of men, just as He did in the case of divorce (Matt. 19:8). It was recognized as a sin on the part of the man, for he had to bring a trespass offering. The woman did not bring an offering.

And when ye shall come into the land, and shall have planted all manner of trees for food, then ye shall count the fruit thereof as uncircumcised: three years shall it be as uncircumcised unto you: it shall not be eaten of.

> But in the fourth year all the fruit thereof shall be holy to
> praise the LORD withal.
>
> And in the fifth year shall ye eat of the fruit thereof, that
> it may yield unto you the increase thereof: I am the LORD
> your God [Lev. 19:23–25].

This law seems strange to those of us who are not dendrologists. We are told, however, that young fruit trees will grow faster and yield better fruit if the buds are nipped off (circumcised) the first few years. The Lord knew that. The spiritual lesson was that the first fruits belong to God. And it taught that "Every good gift and every perfect gift is from above, and cometh down from the Father of lights . . ." (James 1:17).

> Ye shall not eat any thing with the blood: neither shall
> ye use enchantment, nor observe times.
>
> Ye shall not round the corners of your heads, neither
> shalt thou mar the corners of thy beard.
>
> Ye shall not make any cuttings in your flesh for the
> dead, nor print any marks upon you: I am the LORD [Lev.
> 19:26–28].

There are six commandments here that condemn the practices and superstitions of the heathen. They were not to eat flesh with the blood in it. They were not to trim their hair and leave little tufts of it. They were not to act like the heathen when a loved one dies.

> Do not prostitute thy daughter, to cause her to be a
> whore; lest the land fall to whoredom, and the land be-
> come full of wickedness [Lev. 19:29].

This is a condemnation of a heathen practice which prevails to this day among some people. I have read that men in this country go through college with the money their wives earn as harlots. How terrible!

Ye shall keep my sabbaths, and reverence my sanctuary: I am the LORD [Lev. 19:30].

The Sabbath was a sign of the relationship between God and the children of Israel, and it was to be observed strictly. This is brought out in detail in Exodus 31:13–17.

Regard not them that have familiar spirits, neither seek after wizards, to be defiled by them: I am the LORD your God [Lev. 19:31].

This is one of the many warnings against spiritism and demonism. The supernatural and satanic character of this practice is recognized in the Scriptures and rejected.

Thou shalt rise up before the hoary head, and honour the face of the old man, and fear thy God: I am the LORD [Lev. 19:32].

Respect is to be shown old age. This also is repeated in the Scriptures.

And if a stranger sojourn with thee in your land, ye shall not vex him.

But the stranger that dwelleth with you shall be unto you as one born among you, and thou shalt love him as thyself; for ye were strangers in the land of Egypt: I am the LORD your God [Lev. 19:33–34].

The stranger among them was to be treated kindly and was to be loved. He was a reminder to them that they were strangers in Egypt. The stranger was a neighbor.

Ye shall do no unrighteousness in judgment, in meteyard, in weight, or in measure.

> **Just balances, just weights, a just ephah, and a just hin, shall ye have: I am the LORD your God, which brought you out of the land of Egypt [Lev. 19:35–36].**

Business transactions were to be honest. Measures and weights were to be honest. God's children are to be different from others because they represent God even in their business dealings.

> **Therefore shall ye observe all my statutes, and all my judgments, and do them: I am the LORD [Lev. 19:37].**

God is the Lord. That is reason enough for obedience to what He commands. Can you think of anything to add to that?

CHAPTER 20

THEME: *Capital punishment for those who offer their children to Molech; capital punishment for those who practice spiritism; capital punishment for those who curse father or mother; capital punishment for those who commit adultery; certain offenses which require lesser penalty; conclusion to the law of holiness*

D r. Andrew A. Bonar, in his book on Leviticus, calls this chapter "Warnings Against the Sins of the Former Inhabitants." In other words, these were the sins of the Canaanites.

It appears that the death penalty was exacted for breaking any one of the Ten Commandments. Not all of them are listed here under the penal code for the death penalty. Only a few are given as examples. For example, murder is not listed in this chapter, but we learn elsewhere about the death penalty for it. For this reason I infer that the penalty for breaking any of the Ten Commandments was death.

God instituted capital punishment! He is just and righteous, and He applied the death penalty with unsparing severity.

Nowhere in the Word of God is punishment given for the purpose of reforming the criminal. That was not the objective. Punishment of a crime is for the moral good of the people. Punishment of a crime is a deterrent to crime. It will cut down the crime rate. One of the reasons for the spread of lawlessness like a dreadful plague throughout this land is due to the fact that we have weak judges who will not enforce the law.

We hear a great many sob sisters cry about the death penalty. God instituted capital punishment for good and sufficient reasons. There must be the satisfaction of outraged justice. Justice and righteousness demand punishment. The majesty, law, and holiness of God have been outraged, and so crime must be punished.

If you don't believe in the death penalty, let me ask you a question. Do you mean to say that you are better than God? God makes no apology for the death penalty. Listen to Him: "So ye shall not pollute the land wherein ye are: for blood it defileth that land: and the land cannot be cleansed of the blood that is shed therein, but by the blood of him that shed it" (Num. 35:33). Remember that the Books of Matthew and Luke tell us that the blood of Abel cries out from the ground.

Let me ask you another question. Suppose a sadistic criminal took your little child by the heels and dashed his head against a stone. What would you think should be done to him? I'm talking about yours now, not the children of someone else in another state. It's easy to be theoretical and ideal as long as it doesn't involve you. Here in California a man raped a girl and killed the fellow she was with. A crowd was parading at the governor's mansion and parading at the penitentiary, protesting the death sentence. What about the girl? She is in a mental institution, a raving maniac. Her parents believe in capital punishment. I tell you, when you are talking about your own, that changes the color of the picture altogether. God says these people should be punished.

Modern man in his efforts to be soft has abolished the death penalty in the name of this enlightened age. But it still stands in the Word of God as the most humanitarian procedure for the good of all men.

CAPITAL PUNISHMENT FOR THOSE WHO OFFER THEIR CHILDREN TO MOLECH

And the LORD spake unto Moses, saying [Lev. 20:1].

God is speaking to Moses now, not to Aaron or the people. He is speaking to the lawgiver because this is about the penal code. Paul says that those in positions of authority who rule over us do not carry the sword in vain. They are to use it (Rom. 13). A judge has no right to let a sadistic criminal, a psychotic criminal, loose on society to endanger your family and mine.

Someone will say that the electric chair is a mean old chair. That's right, it is. In that day, they were executed by stoning. That's not pretty either. No one has claimed it was pretty. It is an awful thing, a horrible thing. Don't forget, the crime committed is also horrible.

> Again, thou shalt say to the children of Israel, Whoso-
> ever he be of the children of Israel, or of the strangers
> that sojourn in Israel, that giveth any of his seed unto
> Molech; he shall surely be put to death: the people of the
> land shall stone him with stones [Lev. 20:2].

The worship of Molech was savage, satanic, cruel, and brutal. Children were offered as sacrifices to the idol of Molech which was heated red hot. According to historians, the arms of the idol were outstretched and the child was cast "into a gaping hole, full of fire." This was fiendish and demoniacal. What a contrast is Jesus who stretched out His arms to receive little children! "But Jesus said, Suffer little children, and forbid them not, to come unto me: for of such is the kingdom of heaven" (Matt. 19:14). Stoning to death was the penalty for this crime of "giving his seed to Molech," and it is difficult to see how any would oppose the sentence. Stoning is almost too good for them.

Friends, the child brutality today in our land could be curtailed if our judges would punish parents who brutally treat the little ones who can't protect themselves. The judge should protect them.

> And I will set my face against that man, and will cut
> him off from among his people: because he hath given of
> his seed unto Molech, to defile my sanctuary, and to
> profane my holy name [Lev. 20:3].

This is the strongest language possible. "I will set my face against that man." Was this an unpardonable sin? I don't know, but every word is a terrible invective. "I will cut him off from among his people." This sin was a sin against God. It defiles His sanctuary and profanes His holy name. In Ezekiel 23:37–39, we find that the children of Israel did just this, and it was one of the reasons that God's judgment came upon them. Remember that idolatry was high treason in a nation that was a theocracy.

> And if the people of the land do any ways hide their eyes from the man, when he giveth of his seed unto Molech, and kill him not:

> Then I will set my face against that man, and against his family, and will cut him off, and all that go a-whoring after him, to commit whoredom with Molech, from among their people [Lev. 20:4-5].

For a man to remain silent when a neighbor worshiped Molech by offering his child was to make him a partner in crime. To be soft-hearted and soft-headed in executing the penalty made a man guilty. He was to be cut off from the people, which was tantamount to the death penalty.

CAPITAL PUNISHMENT FOR THOSE WHO PRACTICE SPIRITISM

> And the soul that turneth after such as have familiar spirits, and after wizards, to go a-whoring after them, I will even set my face against that soul, and will cut him off from among his people [Lev. 20:6].

This was another practice of the Canaanites who were then in the land. This was false religion which was definitely satanic. Someone may object that it was not the real thing and lacked the supernatural. Frankly, there is supernaturalism manifested in Satan worship. The fact of the matter is that the Lord Jesus Himself warned that there would appear finally an antichrist who would be able to perform miracles, and that, if it were possible, he would deceive the very elect. Satan is a liar and the father of the lie. God says that He will set His face against the soul that turns to this kind of false worship.

> A man also or woman that hath a familiar spirit, or that is a wizard, shall surely be put to death: they shall stone them with stones: their blood shall be upon them [Lev. 20:27].

I bring this verse up into this section as it too deals with satanic super-stition. Demon possession is a reality and has existed in all ages. In this modern age, many cults and "isms" are promoted by those who are demon possessed. This is all the work of Satan. The death penalty was exacted for participating in or practicing these satanic rites of the occult.

Some people are surprised that worshipers of Satan have power. Sure, the devil has power! A departure from the Word of God and a departure from God always leads into error, and this gives rise to the false cults which we find today.

Why did God exact the death penalty for participating in these satanic rites of the occult?

> **Sanctify yourselves therefore, and be ye holy: for I am the Lord your God.**
>
> **And ye shall keep my statutes, and do them: I am the Lord which sanctify you [Lev. 20:7–8].**

These verses offer a good and sufficient reason for the death penalty. The people were to be holy because they belonged to God, and He was holy. Any deviation from this standard was a serious breach of con-duct. To practice the abominations that have been named was to turn from God to Satan. It was spiritual adultery and treason. Today people do not seem to realize how serious that can be. This is God's universe. God is a reality, friends. God's statutes are never to be taken lightly.

CAPITAL PUNISHMENT FOR THOSE WHO CURSE FATHER OR MOTHER

> **For every one that curseth his father or his mother shall be surely put to death: he hath cursed his father or his mother: his blood shall be upon him [Lev. 20:9].**

The fifth commandment was not to be considered of minor impor-tance. In Leviticus 19:3 the Israelite was instructed to fear his father and mother. Now the death penalty was inflicted for cursing father and mother. In Romans 1:31 Paul spoke of those "without natural affection." And we are told that in the last days children will be disobedient to parents, and men will be without natural affection (2 Tim. 3:2–3). This characterized the heathen of the past and will characterize the last days. The punishment stated here is extreme.

We need to mention here that the Bible also offers grace in this regard. The Lord Jesus told the parable of the prodigal son who came home and was received by the father. That is grace. "If we confess our sins, he is faithful and just to forgive us our sins, and to cleanse us from all unrighteousness" (1 John 1:9).

CAPITAL PUNISHMENT FOR THOSE
WHO COMMIT ADULTERY

And the man that committeth adultery with another man's wife, even he that committeth adultery with his neighbour's wife, the adulterer and the adulteress shall surely be put to death.

And the man that lieth with his father's wife hath uncovered his father's nakedness: both of them shall surely be put to death; their blood shall be upon them.

And if a man lie with his daughter-in-law, both of them shall surely be put to death: they have wrought confusion; their blood shall be upon them.

If a man also lie with mankind, as he lieth with a woman, both of them have committed an abomination: they shall surely be put to death; their blood shall be upon them.

And if a man take a wife and her mother, it is wickedness: they shall be burnt with fire, both he and they; that there be no wickedness among you.

And if a man lie with a beast, he shall surely be put to death: and ye shall slay the beast.

> And if a woman approach unto any beast, and lie down
> thereto, thou shalt kill the woman, and the beast: they
> shall surely be put to death; their blood shall be upon
> them [Lev. 20:10–16].

This entire section contains unspeakable and even unbelievable sins. Adultery in every form and shape was punished with death. Sins of sex have caused the most powerful empires to topple. I would say that sex and liquor were the two causes of the fall of Babylon, Egypt, Rome, and France. What a warning this is for our nation!

This is a rebuke against lax morals today. These sins brought down fire and brimstone on Sodom and Gomorrah. These are the sins which cause God to give up a people (Rom. 1:24–28).

In spite of the awful immorality of these sins and the severity of the punishment, the Savior stands ready to forgive any who will come to Him. He put His sacrificial death between this sin and the woman taken in adultery. His sacrificial death atones for you, my friend, if you will come to him for forgiveness.

CERTAIN OFFENSES WHICH REQUIRE
A LESSER PENALTY

> And if a man shall take his sister, his father's daughter,
> or his mother's daughter, and see her nakedness, and
> she see his nakedness; it is a wicked thing: and they
> shall be cut off in the sight of their people: he hath un-
> covered his sister's nakedness; he shall bear his iniq-
> uity.

> And if a man shall lie with a woman having her sick-
> ness, and shall uncover her nakedness; he hath discov-
> ered her fountain, and she hath uncovered the fountain
> of her blood: and both of them shall be cut off from
> among their people.

> And thou shalt not uncover the nakedness of thy
> mother's sister, nor of thy father's sister: for he uncov-
> ereth his near kin: they shall bear their iniquity.

And if a man shall lie with his uncle's wife, he hath uncovered his uncle's nakedness: they shall bear their sin: they shall die childless.

And if a man shall take his brother's wife, it is an unclean thing: he hath uncovered his brother's nakedness; they shall be childless [Lev. 20:17–21].

Incest with a full or half sister was forbidden and the penalty was to be executed publicly. God demanded cleanliness in every detail of his people's lives; especially as it had to do with sexual relations. God forbade sexual relations between those who were near of kin. He did not say that they would not bear children, but that they should die childless—the children would die before the parents who were guilty of this crime.

CONCLUSION TO THE LAW OF HOLINESS

Ye shall therefore keep all my statutes, and all my judgments, and do them: that the land, whither I bring you to dwell therein, spue you not out [Lev. 20:22].

God put the Canaanites out of the land because they committed these awful sins. He warns Israel that He will put them out of the land if they do the same things. God is no respecter of persons. Do you know that their failure to obey God brought on them the Babylonian captivity? Listen to the record: "Manasseh was twelve years old when he began to reign, and reigned fifty and five years in Jerusalem. . . . And he did that which was evil in the sight of the LORD, after the abominations of the heathen, whom the LORD cast out before the children of Israel. . . . And he made his son pass through the fire, and observed times, and used enchantments, and dealt with familiar spirits and wizards: he wrought much wickedness in the sight of the LORD, to provoke him to anger. . . . Manasseh seduced them to do more evil than did the nations whom the LORD destroyed before the children of Israel" (2 Kings 21:1–2, 6, 9).

> **And ye shall not walk in the manners of the nation,
> which I cast out before you: for they committed all these
> things, and therefore I abhorred them [Lev. 20:23].**

This should answer the question as to the justice of God in destroying some of the nations which occupied Palestine. As a result of these sins they were eaten up with social diseases. God forbade His people to take or touch anything in the city of Jericho at the time of the conquest. Evidently venereal diseases had reached epidemic proportions.

> **But I have said unto you, Ye shall inherit their land, and
> I will give it unto you to possess it, a land that floweth
> with milk and honey: I am the LORD your God, which
> have separated you from other people [Lev. 20:24].**

It was a land flowing with milk and honey. Timber covered that land. What happened to it? "Even all nations shall say, Wherefore hath the LORD done thus unto this land? what meaneth the heat of this great anger? Then men shall say, Because they have forsaken the covenant of the LORD God of their fathers, which he made with them when he brought them forth out of the land of Egypt: For they went and served other gods, and worshipped them, gods whom they knew not, and whom he had not given unto them: And the anger of the LORD was kindled against this land, to bring upon it all the curses that are written in this book: And the LORD rooted them out of their land in anger, and in wrath, and in great indignation, and cast them into another land, as it is this day" (Deut. 29:24–28). They are planting trees over there today. When I was there, I set out five trees; one for each member of my family, one for the church that I served, and one for a Jewish friend.

> **Ye shall therefore put difference between clean beasts
> and unclean, and between unclean fowls and clean: and
> ye shall not make your souls abominable by beast, or by
> fowl, or by any manner of living thing that creepeth on**

the ground, which I have separated from you as unclean [Lev. 20:25].

God reviews the statutes which were to make His people a different and a holy people. He began with their diet, and He concludes with it.

And ye shall be holy unto me: for I the LORD am holy, and have severed you from other people, that ye should be mine [Lev. 20:26].

They are out of the land because they did not obey God. They were to be a holy nation like unto their God who is holy. "But," you may say, "they are in the land." May I ask how they are getting along? They have had trouble every minute they have been back in the land. Do you know what the problem is? They went back to the land but they did not return to God. When they do return to God—which they will do someday—then there will be blessing in that land. God hasn't changed His mind, friends.

This should be a lesson to us and to our nation. God is high and holy, and He demands holiness. This is the key to Leviticus.

CHAPTER 21

THEME: Defilement of priesthood prevented in human kinship and friendship; disqualifications for priestly function

We have been studying the law as directed to the people from chapter 11 through chapter 20. Now we come to the law for the personal purity of the priests. This is found in chapters 21 and 22. We will find a certain amount of repetition here.

It had been God's original intention that the entire nation should be a kingdom of priests (Exod. 19:5-6). Their disobedience in the matter of the golden calf destroyed the possibility of the realization of a perfect and ideal society. In the Millennium, the perfect society will be attained. Then the entire nation of Israel will be the priests here on the earth for the earthly people, the gentile nations. Through the Millennium and through eternity, there are the three groups of the human family: (1) the church of Jesus Christ in the New Jerusalem, (2) the nation Israel here on this earth, (3) the saved Gentiles on this earth.

After Israel's failure, God chose only one tribe to be the priests, the tribe of Levi. In Israel, therefore, there were the congregation, the priesthood, and the high priest. The higher position required a higher obligation. The greater responsibility demanded a higher way of life.

The church today is called a royal priesthood. Every believer is a priest and has access to the throne of grace today. Every believer-priest is required to live a holy life which is possible only by the power of the indwelling Holy Spirit. "And above all things have fervent charity among yourselves: for charity shall cover the multitude of sins. Use hospitality one to another without grudging. As every man hath received the gift, even so minister the same one to another, as good stewards of the manifold grace of God. If any man speak, let him speak as the oracles of God; if any man minister, let him do it as of the ability which God giveth: that God in all things may be glorified through Jesus Christ, to whom be praise and dominion for ever and ever. Amen" (1 Pet. 4:8–11). He also said, "But ye are a chosen generation, a royal priesthood, an holy nation, a peculiar people; that ye should shew forth the praises of him who hath called you out of darkness into his marvellous light: which in time past were not a people, but are now the people of God: which had not obtained mercy, but now have obtained mercy" (1 Pet. 2:9–10).

As God's people we are called to a higher way of life. "This I say therefore, and testify in the Lord, that ye henceforth walk not as other Gentiles walk, in the vanity of their mind. . . . That ye put off concerning the former conversation the old man, which is corrupt according to the deceitful lusts; and be renewed in the spirit of your mind; and that ye put on the new man, which after God is created in righteousness and true holiness" (Eph. 4:17, 22–24). The child of God is saved by grace and has been called to a high place in his life.

A believer should be careful about accepting an office in the church. If he does become an officer, he should measure up to that responsibility. I have very little patience with men who accept an office in the church and then say they are not able to come to the midweek service or come on Sunday night. Well, my brother, you should not have accepted the office. Responsibility, you see, comes through privilege. It is a privilege to serve the Lord in an office. You have been elevated. Then live up to it.

Jesus Christ is our Great High Priest and He measured up to His office. "For such an high priest became us, who is holy, harmless, undefiled, separate from sinners, and made higher than the heavens; who needeth not daily, as those high priests, to offer up sacrifice, first for his own sins, and then for the people's: for this he did once, when he offered up himself. For the law maketh men high priests which have infirmity; but the word of the oath, which was since the law, maketh the Son, who is consecrated for evermore" (Heb. 7:26–28). The Lord Jesus Christ is both the priest and the sacrifice. He offered Himself.

The priests and the high priest now come under the purview of the law. Let us look at it.

DEFILEMENT OF PRIESTHOOD PREVENTED IN HUMAN KINSHIP AND FRIENDSHIP

And the Lᴏʀᴅ said unto Moses, Speak unto the priests the sons of Aaron, and say unto them, There shall none be defiled for the dead among his people:

But for his kin, that is near unto him, that is, for his mother, and for his father, and for his son, and for his daughter, and for his brother.

And for his sister a virgin, that is nigh unto him, which hath had no husband: for her may he be defiled [Lev. 21:1–3].

Moses is to address this section to the priests. Death is a penalty of sin, and the idea is that they are not to be contaminated with sin. Physical contact with the dead brings defilement. The priest was permitted to defile himself for close relatives. These listed here are all blood relations and by nature close to the priest. He must be permitted to express his feelings of sympathy and grief as a priest of God. He must be a type of Jesus who could weep at the grave of Lazarus and was touched with the feelings of our infirmities. He was not, however, permitted to defile himself for the dead of any others. He could mourn in his heart, but was denied physical contact.

But he shall not defile himself, being a chief man among his people, to profane himself [Lev. 21:4].

The office he occupied required of him a stricter separation than any common man among the people.

There are places that I don't go, not because they are wrong, but because I am an ordained minister and I don't want to give any occasion for offense to anyone. I believe that pastors, deacons, elders, Sunday school teachers, and all others who serve in the church, should be extremely careful about where they go, what they do and say. God is

going to hold you and me more responsible if He has placed us in a
position of responsibility.

> **They shall not make baldness upon their head, neither
> shall they shave off the corner of their beard, nor make
> any cuttings in their flesh [Lev. 21:5].**

This was something the heathen did, and they did it as an act of
mourning for the dead. The priest was not to practice these supersti-
tious, pagan practices that were all around him.

> **They shall be holy unto their God, and not profane the
> name of their God: for the offerings of the LORD made by
> fire, and the bread of their God, they do offer: therefore
> they shall be holy [Lev. 21:6].**

Their mourning was to befit those who were cupbearers of the King,
"the bread of their God." Their position demanded dignity and re-
straint as God's representatives. The same applies to God's representatives in the church today: "For a bishop must be blameless, as the
steward of God; not selfwilled, not soon angry, not given to wine, no
striker, not given to filthy lucre; but a lover of hospitality, a lover of
good men, sober, just, holy, temperate" (Titus 1:7–8).

> **They shall not take a wife that is a whore, or profane;
> neither shall they take a woman put away from her hus-
> band: for he is holy unto his God.**
>
> **Thou shalt sanctify him therefore; for he offereth the
> bread of thy God: he shall be holy unto thee: for I the
> LORD, which sanctify you, am holy [Lev. 21:7–8].**

This refers to his personal and private life, and in that, too, he is to
reveal the holiness of God because of his position. He shall not marry
a harlot, profane woman, or a divorced person. The reason given is
because he is serving God—"offereth the bread of thy God."

The priest is a type of Christ. Also the body of believers, called the *bride* of Christ, is to be cleansed before she is presented to Him without spot or wrinkle (Eph. 5:26–27).

The church leader is to be an example to others in this particular matter. May I say right here that I get many letters from both men and women who were divorced before they were saved. Some of the men want to enter the ministry and the women wish to become missionaries. I know one cannot generalize about these things, but I do want to say that I think it is almost sinful the way certain innocent people who had an unfortunate experience in their lives—many of them before they were saved—are shut out from an office because of that past experience in which they were not guilty at all. I encourage these people to go ahead and prepare for the ministry or the mission field. But I warn them also to be prepared to weather the criticism of some "saint" who thinks he is speaking for God. Also, they will find certain churches that will shut them out. Yet I encourage them to go ahead with their preparation because there will be a place for them. And there is. We need to recognize that in this day there are a great many people who are the innocent victims of divorce.

Another thing we need to recognize is that the wife of a pastor is not an assistant pastor. She is simply the wife of the pastor; that is the role she is to fill. She must be the kind of person who would be a credit to the office that the man occupies. It is not required of her that she must play the piano and the organ, sing in the choir, lead the missionary society, and on and on.

And the daughter of any priest, if she profane herself by playing the whore, she profaneth her father: she shall be burnt with fire [Lev. 21:9].

Why? Because of the position of her father. She was to receive the severest of penalties if she disgraced the office of her father.

And he that is the high priest among his brethren, upon whose head the anointing oil was poured, and that is

consecrated to put on the garments, shall not uncover
his head, nor rend his clothes;

Neither shall he go in to any dead body, nor defile himself for his father, or for his mother;

Neither shall he go out of the sanctuary, nor profane the
sanctuary of his God: for the crown of the anointing oil
of his God is upon him: I am the LORD [Lev. 21:10–12].

This is the first mention of the high priest. As God's anointed priest,
he is to be separated unto the Lord. He was to wear the crown on
which were inscribed the words "Holiness unto the Lord" as a continual reminder of who he is, whose he is, and whom he serves.

He is not to rend his holy garments. He was not to be a violent man.
At the trial of Jesus this law was broken when the high priest emotion-
ally tore his clothes (Matt. 26:65). Neither was the high priest to at-
tend the funeral of either his father or mother. The anointing oil had
been poured upon him, and he must be totally dedicated to God and
separated from sin because of his position.

The Lord Jesus Christ had the anointing oil poured upon Him and
He came to do the Father's will even unto death. He demands just such
a dedication on the part of His followers.

And he shall take a wife in her virginity.

A widow, or a divorced woman, or profane, or an harlot, these shall he not take: but he shall take a virgin of
his own people to wife.

Neither shall he profane his seed among his people: for I
the LORD do sanctify him [Lev. 21:13–15].

His wife too must measure up to the position of the holy office. He is
forbidden to marry a harlot, a profane or a divorced woman.

DISQUALIFICATIONS FOR PRIESTLY FUNCTION

The following verses list disqualifications for the priestly function. It includes blindness, lameness, flat nose, dwarfism, scabs, and other deformities and blemishes.

And the LORD spake unto Moses, saying.

Speak unto Aaron, saying, Whosoever he be of thy seed in their generations that hath any blemish, let him not approach to offer the bread of his God.

For whatsoever man he be that hath a blemish, he shall not approach: a blind man, or a lame, or he that hath a flat nose, or any thing superfluous.

Or, a man that is brokenfooted, or brokenhanded,

Or crookbacked, or a dwarf, or that hath a blemish in his eye, or be scurvy, or scabbed, or hath his stones broken;

No man that hath a blemish of the seed of Aaron the priest shall come nigh to offer the offerings of the LORD made by fire: he hath a blemish; he shall not come nigh to offer the bread of his God [Lev. 21:16-21].

Why should this be? Just as no sacrifice was to be offered that had a blemish, by the same token no priest was to serve in the tabernacle if he had a blemish. Both the offering and the offerer represent Christ and there is no blemish in Him, either in His person or in His work. Christ is the perfect High Priest. There is no blemish in Him but rather beauty and glory and excellency.

He shall eat the bread of his God, both of the most holy, and of the holy.

> Only he shall not go unto the vail, nor come nigh unto
> the altar, because he hath a blemish; that he profane not
> my sanctuaries: for I the LORD do sanctify them [Lev.
> 21:22–23].

Although those with a blemish were forbidden to serve, they were not
shut out from the table of the Lord. God provided for them. This is in
contrast to the treatment the pagan world gave the unfit.

There is a spiritual lesson for us here. There are many believers
who have some serious handicap either physically, morally, ethically,
or spiritually. This would bar them from certain forms of service, yet
they are genuine saints of God who have all the rights and privileges
of believers in every respect.

When I was studying for the ministry, I taught a young fellow in
Sunday school who was in junior high school at the time. He was a
marvelous athlete, but he had a cleft palate with a speech impediment. He came to me one day and told me that he would like to be a
minister. Now, how do you talk to a young fellow like that? I tried to
explain to him that he was a wonderful athlete, but that his speech
was a handicap and suggested he find something in Christian work
which would not require public speaking. I've followed this man
through the years. He became a football coach at a college. His influence for Christ was as great or greater than any minister's. They
learned to admire this man as an athlete and then, with his speech
impediment, he would tell them about Jesus Christ and it made a real
impact upon them.

CHAPTER 22

THEME: Defilement of the priesthood through disease, diet, and the dead; discernment of the offerings brought by the people

DEFILEMENT OF THE PRIESTHOOD THROUGH DISEASE, DIET, AND THE DEAD

And the Lord spake unto Moses, saying,

Speak unto Aaron and to his sons, that they separate themselves from the holy things of the children of Israel, and that they profane not my holy name in those things which they hallow unto me: I am the Lord [Lev. 22:1–2].

There was to be a separation of the sacred and the secular. Aaron was not to bring the things of the tabernacle home with him. The lesson for us is that we are not to treat the sacred and holy things of God as if they were commonplace.

Say unto them, Whosoever he be of all your seed among your generations, that goeth unto the holy things, which the children of Israel hallow unto the Lord, having his uncleanness upon him, that soul shall be cut off from my presence: I am the Lord [Lev. 22:3].

The priest is not to go about his office in a careless and slipshod manner. God requires that he should be put out of the office of the priesthood if he does that. I believe there is a spiritual application for the believer today. "For if we would judge ourselves, we should not be judged. But when we are judged, we are chastened of the Lord, that we should not be condemned with the world" (1 Cor. 11:31–32).

God proceeds to enumerate all manner of uncleanness which would disqualify the priest from carrying out his priestly duties.

> What man soever of the seed of Aaron is a leper, or hath
> a running issue; he shall not eat of the holy things, until
> he be clean. And whoso toucheth any thing that is un-
> clean by the dead, or a man whose seed goeth from him;
>
> Or whosoever toucheth any creeping thing, whereby he
> may be made unclean, or a man of whom he may take
> uncleanness, whatsoever uncleanness he hath;
>
> The soul which hath touched any such shall be unclean
> until even, and shall not eat of the holy things, unless he
> wash his flesh with water.
>
> And when the sun is down, he shall be clean, and shall
> afterward eat of the holy things; because it is his food.
>
> That which dieth of itself, or is torn with beasts, he shall
> not eat to defile himself therewith: I am the LORD.
>
> They shall therefore keep mine ordinance, lest they bear
> sin for it, and die therefore, if they profane it: I the LORD
> do sanctify them [Lev. 22:4–9].

The priests were to be holy in their relationships in their homes, in
their social contacts, in their business contacts, in anything where
they touched the world. The priests were set apart to be holy unto the
Lord. They were to be an example to others. Some of the things mentioned are the same as those given for all of Israel. The priest had no
special privileges. Uncleanness in the common man and uncleanness
in the priest were to be ceremonially cleansed. The private life of the
priest must match his public office and service.

> There shall no stranger eat of the holy thing: a sojourner
> of the priest, or an hired servant, shall not eat of the holy
> thing [Lev. 22:10].

The priest must preserve the sanctity of the tabernacle by excluding
the stranger. Only the sons of God can worship God.

> But if the priest buy any soul with his money, he shall eat of it, and he that is born in his house: they shall eat of his meat.
>
> If the priest's daughter also be married unto a stranger, she may not eat of an offering of the holy things.
>
> But if the priest's daughter be a widow, or divorced, and have no child, and is returned unto her father's house, as in her youth, she shall eat of her father's meat: but there shall no stranger eat thereof [Lev. 22:11–13].

The verses go on to explain that only those who belong to the priest, who were born in his house, can eat of his meat. If a priest's daughter married a Gentile, she was excluded from access to the holy things. If she were widowed or divorced and returned to her father's house, she could eat her father's meat. The prodigal son or daughter may return home and find a welcome.

> And if a man eat of the holy thing unwittingly, then he shall put the fifth part thereof unto it, and shall give it unto the priest with the holy thing.
>
> And they shall not profane the holy things of the children of Israel, which they offer unto the LORD;
>
> Or suffer them to bear the iniquity of trespass, when they eat their holy things: for I the LORD do sanctify them [Lev. 22:14–16].

Ignorance of the law affords no excuse. The man who eats of the holy things unwittingly is guilty. A fine is expected of him. This placed an added responsibility upon the priests to guard the holy place.

The unbelieving world gains its impression of the church from the members of the church. Indifference and irreverence is detected immediately by the outside unbeliever, and his attitude and conduct is governed accordingly. The Lord Jesus said, "Woe unto the world because of offences! for it must needs be that offences come; but woe to that man by whom the offence cometh" (Matt. 18:7).

DISCERNMENT OF THE OFFERINGS
BROUGHT BY THE PEOPLE

And the LORD spake unto Moses, saying,

Speak unto Aaron, and to his sons, and unto all the children of Israel, and say unto them, Whatsoever he be of the house of Israel, or of the strangers in Israel, that will offer his oblation for all his vows, and for all his freewill offerings, which they will offer unto the LORD for a burnt offering:

Ye shall offer at your own will a male without blemish, of the beeves, of the sheep, or of the goats.

But whatsoever hath a blemish, that shall ye not offer: for it shall not be acceptable for you [Lev. 22:17–20].

This section contains rules and regulations for the people in bringing their offerings, and these rules must be strictly enforced by the priests. The regulations apply to the people, but the enforcement applies to the priests. No offering with a blemish was to be permitted because the offerings pointed to Christ. Any departure from this was to lower the concept of the person of Christ and the holy demands of God.

And whosoever offereth a sacrifice of peace offerings unto the LORD to accomplish his vow, or a freewill offering in beeves or sheep, it shall be perfect to be accepted; there shall be no blemish therein.

Blind, or broken, or maimed, or having a wen, or scurvy, or scabbed, ye shall not offer these unto the LORD, nor make an offering by fire of them upon the altar unto the LORD.

> Either a bullock or a lamb that hath any thing superfluous or lacking in his parts, that mayest thou offer for a freewill offering; but for a vow it shall not be accepted.
>
> Ye shall not offer unto the LORD that which is bruised, or crushed, or broken, or cut; neither shall ye make any offering thereof in your land.
>
> Neither from a stranger's hand shall ye offer the bread of your God of any of these; because their corruption is in them, and blemishes be in them: they shall not be accepted for you.
>
> And the LORD spake unto Moses, saying,
>
> When a bullock, or a sheep, or a goat, is brought forth, then it shall be seven days under the dam; and from the eighth day and thenceforth it shall be accepted for an offering made by fire unto the LORD.
>
> And whether it be cow or ewe, ye shall not kill it and her young both in one day [Lev. 22:21–28].

Natural deformity in an animal as well as bruises and cuts and broken bones comprised the blemishes. Any of these should make them reject the animal as an offering. No stranger was to make an offering. And any offering animal was to be at least seven days old. Seven represents completion—it was to have lived a complete cycle.

It was at this point of offering animals without blemish that Israel failed miserably. They brought that which was torn and lame and sick for their offerings and God called forth from the prophets a denunciation of their offerings. We find this in Malachi 1:6–14.

> And when ye will offer a sacrifice of thanksgiving unto the LORD, offer it at your own will.
>
> On the same day it shall be eaten up; ye shall leave none of it until the morrow: I am the LORD [Lev. 22:29–30].

The offering was to be a freewill offering. This type of offering must represent the Father who gave His Son in love and the Son who came ". . . for the joy that was set before him . . ." (Heb. 12:2). The offering must be eaten the same day. No opportunity must be allowed for the slightest bit of corruption.

> **Therefore shall ye keep my commandments, and do them: I am the LORD.**
>
> **Neither shall ye profane my holy name; but I will be hallowed among the children of Israel: I am the LORD which hallow you,**
>
> **That brought you out of the land of Egypt, to be your God: I am the LORD [Lev. 22:31–33].**

They were to be a witness for God. They were not to go as witnesses to the ends of the earth as you and I have been called to do today. They were called to serve God as a nation. As they did this, the whole world would come to Jerusalem. God's holy name was to be represented in every act of worship.

What was to be the motivation for their obedience? Dr. Andrew A. Bonar gives five reasons:

(1) "I am the Lord"
(2) "I will be hallowed among the children of Israel"
(3) "I am the Lord which hallow you"
(4) "I am the Lord which brought you out of Egypt"
(5) "Your God."

"I am the Lord which hallow you." There is liberty for the believer today, but liberty does not grant license. The holiness and righteousness of God must be zealously maintained in all our worship.

"I am the Lord which brought you out of Egypt." God has saved you, my friend. God saves you by grace. He didn't save you with the idea of exacting commensurate work from you. Then it wouldn't be grace. I do not agree with the words of the song, "I gave My life for thee, what hast thou done for Me?" Grace does not demand payment. But let me ask you a question. Do you love Him? Do you *want* to serve

Him? The wife doesn't fix a birthday dinner for her husband because it is her duty. She does it because she loves the old boy! And the true believer will serve God because he loves Him.

"I am the LORD which hallow you, that brought you out of the land of Egypt, *to be your God.*" Is He your God, my friend? If He is, then you represent Him. The world is reading you. Remember the little poem:

> The Gospel is written a chapter a day
> By the deeds that you do and words that you say.
> Men read what you say whether faithless or true.
> Say, what is the Gospel according to you?

Men are not reading the Bible today. They are reading you and me. What are they reading in you, my friend?

CHAPTER 23

THEME: *The holy seasons of the Sabbath; the holy season of Passover; the holy season of Unleavened Bread; the holy season of Firstfruits; the holy season of Pentecost; the holy season of Trumpets; the holy season of the great Day of Atonement; the holy season of Tabernacles*

This is a remarkable chapter of God's solemn festivals. The holy holidays were times of joy. There was mourning on only one of them, the great Day of Atonement. The others were to be times of joy and rejoicing. God never wanted a weeping people to come before Him; He wanted a rejoicing people. These festivals provide God's calendar for all time.

John Peter Lange gives the meaning of the so-called feasts as "a fixed, appointed time." It is sometimes translated a "set time." Perhaps "holy seasons" would be the most appropriate translation.

Details for most of these feasts are given elsewhere in Scripture. Here they are given in an orderly and purposeful arrangement. There are seven feasts, excluding the Sabbath Day, which is given first. The Sabbath Day was not a feast day, but is included because it furnishes the yardstick for the measuring of time. The number seven is as prominent in this chapter as in the Book of Revelation. It is the dimension of time.

The Sabbath Day is the seventh day. Pentecost is the feast of the seventh week; the seventh new moon with its following Day of Atonement and Feast of Tabernacles is the feast of the seventh month. In the twenty-fifth chapter we will have occasion to consider the sabbatic year and the year of Jubilee, all adjusted to the number seven. There were seven days of unleavened bread, and seven days of dwelling in tabernacles in the Feast of Tabernacles.

These days of holy convocation served a twofold purpose: a practical purpose and a prophetic purpose. On the practical plane they

served both a social and commercial purpose. They brought the
twelve tribes together in worship and fellowship. All males were required to go to Jerusalem to worship on three occasions: at the feasts
of Passover, Pentecost, and Tabernacles (Deut. 16:16). You can see that
this would have a tendency to unite the nation and knit the tribes together. The people would come from all sections of the kingdom and
exchange ideas as well as merchandise. Failure to follow these instructions was one of the contributing factors in dividing the nation
into northern and southern kingdoms.

Most of these feasts were geared into the agricultural life of the
land, especially the harvesting of the crops. This was especially true
of the feasts of Firstfruits, Pentecost, and Tabernacles. This brought
the worship of Jehovah down to the grain field, the vineyard, and the
fig orchard. Praise to God was united with the work of the people. The
sweat of their brow became a sacred thing.

The primary purpose of these feast days was to give a prophetic
picture of all future time. Each one of these feasts has found or will
find a fulfillment in time. Most of them have been fulfilled. We will
point this out as we go along.

We are no longer to observe days and seasons because Christ has
fulfilled them. "Let no man therefore judge you in meat, or in drink,
or in respect of an holyday, or of the new moon, or of the sabbath days:
which are a shadow of things to come; but the body is of Christ" (Col.
2:16–17).

I should mention that all the festivals and observances are not included in this chapter. The Sabbatic year and the year of Jubilee are
found in chapter 25, and the New Moons in Numbers 28:11–15.

THE HOLY SEASONS OF THE SABBATH

And the LORD spake unto Moses, saying,

**Speak unto the children of Israel, and say unto them,
Concerning the feasts of the LORD, which ye shall proclaim to be holy convocations, even these are my feasts.**

> **Six days shall work be done: but the seventh day is the sabbath of rest, an holy convocation; ye shall do no work therein: it is the sabbath of the LORD in all your dwellings [Lev. 23:1-3].**

If you will notice, as we go through this book, God always directs His instructions to certain people, and it is well to note the ones to whom He is directing the instructions. He tells Moses as the lawgiver, and he in turn is to tell the people. Even though the feasts will involve the tabernacle, the priests are not specifically mentioned. The people were to come together, and the feasts were to fit into the yearly calendar of Israel.

Passover—the crucifixion and death of Christ

Unleavened Bread—the fellowship we have with Christ because of His death

Firstfruits—the resurrection of Christ

Pentecost—the beginning of the church

Trumpets—Israel brought back into the land (future)

Great Day of Atonement—the work of Christ upon the Cross for us

Tabernacles—the time when Israel is in the land (future)

The weekly Sabbath cannot properly be labeled one of the feast days. It is pre-Mosaic and goes back to the original creation. It was repeated to Israel, and in Deuteronomy an additional reason for its observance is given. "And remember that thou wast a servant in the land of Egypt, and that the LORD thy God brought thee out thence through a mighty hand and by a stretched out arm: therefore the LORD thy God commanded thee to keep the sabbath day" (Deut. 5:15).

When they were slaves down in Egypt, they had to work every day.

The Sabbath Day is tied in with their deliverance. Now that they have been delivered from Egypt, they are to set aside one day to worship God. There is to be cessation from all labor and activity.

When the early church set aside a day of the week to come together, they chose Sunday, the first day of the week, because it was the day our Lord came back from the dead. That is the day full deliverance was given to us. "Who was delivered for our offences, and was raised again for our justification" (Rom. 4:25). The Sabbath Day belongs to the old creation. We belong to the new creation. ". . . if any man be in Christ, he is a new creature [creation] . . ." (2 Cor. 5:17). We honor Christ by setting aside the first day of the week.

The Sabbath was a yardstick of time for Israel. It spoke of cessation from all labor and activity and looked forward to a new week when there would be a new creation. It was also prophetic in that it looked forward to redemption. Man lost his rest in the first creation, but now rest is his through redemption. "There remaineth therefore a rest to the people of God. For he that is entered into his rest, he also hath ceased from his own works, as God did from his. Let us labour therefore to enter into that rest, lest any man fall after the same example of unbelief" (Heb. 4:9–11). Our rest comes through redemption and redemption only. There is a rest for the people of God. What is it? Our sins are forgiven. "Come unto me, all ye that labour and are heavy laden, and I will give you rest" (Matt. 11:28). Rest and redemption are the twofold aspect of the Sabbath Day.

The Sabbath Day was not a feast day. It is geared to the week and not to the year. It was not a feast, but a set time.

THE HOLY SEASON OF PASSOVER

These are the feasts of the LORD, even holy convocations, which ye shall proclaim in their seasons.

In the fourteenth day of the first month at even is the LORD's passover [Lev. 23:4–5].

The description of the feast was given to us back in Exodus 12, but here it is placed in the calendar of God. This verse makes it clear that the feasts begin properly with the Passover and not the Sabbath. In Exodus 12:2 God said, "This month shall be unto you the beginning of months: it shall be the first month of the year to you." This holy season represents the sacrificial death of Christ and the value of His blood. "Purge out therefore the old leaven, that ye may be a new lump, as ye are unleavened. For even Christ our passover is sacrificed for us" (1 Cor. 5:7).

The Passover originated in the historical event of the last plague in Egypt by the slaying of the firstborn. Israel was instructed to slay a lamb and put the blood of the lamb on the doorposts of their homes. They were to stay inside, roast the lamb, and eat it. The angel of death would pass over every door which was marked with the blood. When we get to Numbers 9, we will find that Israel kept the Passover when they were encamped at Mount Sinai.

The Passover was brought to its fulfillment the night of the arrest of the Lord Jesus Christ after He had observed the Passover with His disciples, and had instituted a new feast on the dying embers of the old. Then we see the Lamb slain in Revelation 5:6. I think the Passover will be observed again in the Kingdom. "For I say unto you, I will not any more eat thereof, until it be fulfilled in the kingdom of God" (Luke 22:16).

THE HOLY SEASON OF UNLEAVENED BREAD

And on the fifteenth day of the same month is the feast of unleavened bread unto the LORD: seven days ye must eat unleavened bread.

In the first day ye shall have an holy convocation: ye shall do no servile work therein.

But ye shall offer an offering made by fire unto the LORD seven days: in the seventh day is an holy convocation: ye shall do no servile work therein [Lev. 23:6–8].

Although this is considered a separate feast, it is closely aligned with the Passover. Passover was observed one day, and the next day—

the first day of the week—began the Feast of Unleavened Bread. Its historical origin is in direct connection with the Passover (Exod. 12:14–28). Unleavened bread was to be eaten for seven days beginning on the day after Passover. In Matthew and Mark the Passover and Unleavened Bread are considered as one feast.

Leaven here, as elsewhere, is the symbol of evil. The unleavened bread speaks of fellowship with Christ based on His redemption and maintained by the holy walk of the believer (1 Cor. 5:7–8).

No servile work was to be done. On those days the participants were to rest from their daily occupations. There were to be offerings made by fire which refer to burnt offerings, meal offerings, and sin offerings. The first and the seventh days of the week of Unleavened Bread were the particular days of an "holy convocation."

The Passover speaks of the death of Christ for our sins. After that, we are now to maintain fellowship with Him on the basis of the fact that He died for us. We are to remain clean by confessing our sins as we go along. Our Lord said to His men, ". . . If I wash thee not, thou hast no part with me" (John 13:8). It signifies that the value of the blood of Christ continues for the believer after he is saved. "But if we walk in the light, as he is in the light, we have fellowship one with another, and the blood of Jesus Christ his Son cleanseth us from all sin" (1 John 1:7). The blood of Jesus Christ *keeps on* keeping us clean. That is the meaning of the feast of Mazzoth, Unleavened Bread.

THE HOLY SEASON OF FIRSTFRUITS

And the LORD **spake unto Moses, saying,**

Speak unto the children of Israel, and say unto them, When ye be come into the land which I give unto you, and shall reap the harvest thereof, then ye shall bring a sheaf of the firstfruits of your harvest unto the priest:

And he shall wave the sheaf before the LORD**, to be accepted for you: on the morrow after the sabbath the priest shall wave it [Lev. 23:9–11].**

This feast could not be observed until Israel got out of the wilderness and into the Promised Land. When they had sowed their grain in the land, they were to watch for the first heading of the barley. When they would see a stalk here and there, they would cut each one down and put them together to make a sheaf. This was then brought to the tabernacle, and the priest would offer it to the Lord.

The exact day that he did this is not stated. It may have been the first day of Unleavened Bread or the last day of that feast. The important item to note is that it was done on the first day of the week. This is so important because Christ is called the firstfruits. "But now is Christ risen from the dead, and become the firstfruits of them that slept" (1 Cor. 15:20). "But every man in his own order: Christ the firstfruits; afterward they that are Christ's at his coming" (1 Cor. 15:23). The time of His resurrection is clearly stated in Matthew 28:1: "In the end of the sabbath, as it began to dawn toward the first day of the week, came Mary Magdalene and the other Mary to see the sepulchre." On the first day of the week, Christ, "the firstfruits" was resurrected from the dead.

Someday the church will be included in resurrection, but so far He is the only One who has been raised in a glorified body. At the rapture of the church, we shall all rise. There will be a coming out of the graves just as Christ did. He is the firstfruits, afterwards they that are Christ's at His coming. "Verily, verily, I say unto you, Except a corn of wheat fall into the ground and die, it abideth alone: but if it die, *it bringeth forth much fruit*" (John 12:24, italics mine).

You see, the offering of the firstfruits indicated that there would be a harvest to follow. Believers are that harvest.

> **And ye shall offer that day when ye wave the sheaf an he lamb without blemish of the first year for a burnt offering unto the LORD.**

> **And the meat offering thereof shall be two tenth deals of fine flour mingled with oil, an offering made by fire**

**unto the LORD for a sweet savour: and the drink offering
thereof shall be of wine, the fourth part of an hin.**

**And ye shall eat neither bread, nor parched corn, nor
green ears, until the selfsame day that ye have brought
an offering unto your God: it shall be a statute for ever
throughout your generations in all your dwellings [Lev.
23:12-14].**

Offerings accompanied the celebration of this day. No sin offering was
included because that was included in the death of Christ—that is
where He settled the sin question. These offerings are a sweet savor.
"For he hath made him to be sin for us, who knew no sin; that we
might be made the righteousness of God in him" (2 Cor. 5:21).
". . . because I live, ye shall live also" (John 14:19). This is a glorious
truth that we have here.

The new crop of grain could not be enjoyed until this offering was
waved before Jehovah. For the believer, the death and resurrection of
Christ brings us into new relationships and blessings. "Therefore if
any man be in Christ, he is a new creature: old things are passed
away; behold, all things are become new" (2 Cor. 5:17). That doesn't
mean that just a few habits change. It means we are taken out of the
old Adam, and we are joined to the Lord Jesus Christ. Now we have a
new purpose, a new goal, a new joy, and new life—and that would
affect a few old habits, would it not? He makes all things new.

THE HOLY SEASON OF PENTECOST

Notice the orderly, chronological sequence that we have here. Pass-
over tells us that Christ, our Passover, is sacrificed for us. Unleavened
Bread is sharing the things of Christ, fellowship with Him. Then
Firstfruits signifies Christ's resurrection, the firstfruits from the dead.
Now we come to Pentecost.

**And ye shall count unto you from the morrow after the
sabbath, from the day that ye brought the sheaf of the
wave offering; seven sabbaths shall be complete:**

Even unto the morrow after the seventh sabbath shall ye number fifty days; and ye shall offer a new meat offering unto the LORD [Lev. 23:15–16].

There are several things we need to note about Pentecost because there is so much being made of it today that is absolutely unscriptural. The Feast of Pentecost always fell on the first day of the week. They counted seven Sabbaths, which would be seven weeks or forty-nine days, then the fiftieth day, the day after the seventh Sabbath, the first day of the week, was Pentecost. This was fifty days after the offering of the wave sheaf of firstfruits.

The church was born on the first day of the week. It was on the first day of the week that our Lord arose. Doesn't that tell us something? Wouldn't it be rather odd for the church to go back and observe the old Sabbath which belonged to the old creation when the church is a new creation? When the church meets on the first day of the week, we are celebrating our Lord's resurrection and the birthday of the church. This festival is also called the Feast of Weeks.

The typical meaning of Pentecost is not left to man's speculation. "And when the day of Pentecost was fully come, they were all with one accord in one place. . . . And they were all filled with the Holy Ghost, and began to speak with other tongues, as the Spirit gave them utterance" (Acts 2:1, 4). "When the day of Pentecost was fully come" doesn't mean at twelve noon or at six in the evening. "The day of Pentecost was fully come" means the fulfillment of that for which it was given in Leviticus. It denotes the coming of the Holy Spirit to baptize believers into the body of Christ and to begin the calling out of the church. Pentecost is the birthday of the church.

It was fifty days after the resurrection of Christ that the Holy Spirit came. God was running according to His calendar and on time.

They were to offer a new meal offering. That is a type of the church. The church is something new. Christ didn't say that He would give us an old garment and patch it up. He came to bring a brand new robe of righteousness. To be in Christ is to be clothed with His righteousness. That is how God sees us.

We need to note the time sequence. After the resurrection of the

Lord Jesus, He showed Himself alive for forty days. Then, just before He ascended into heaven, He said to His own that they should not depart from Jerusalem, but wait for the promise of the Father. He told them they should be endued with power from on high (Luke 24:49). In Acts 1:5 it states: ". . . but ye shall be baptized with the Holy Ghost not many days hence." Ten days later, on the day of Pentecost, the Spirit of God came upon them.

> **Ye shall bring out of your habitations two wave loaves of two tenth deals: they shall be of fine flour; they shall be baken with leaven; they are the firstfruits unto the LORD [Lev. 23:17].**

Do you notice anything startling about this verse? We have said that leaven is the principle of evil and that it was not to be in the offerings. Here is the exception. This is typifying the church, and it is a new offering in that it is a meal offering with leaven included. What does it mean? It means there is evil in the church. This is obvious to the most casual observer.

I was a pastor for forty years. I have served in four different states from the Atlantic to the Pacific. I have been in some wonderful churches, and I look back on those years with a real joy. I've had wonderful fellowship with the members of these churches. They have loved me and I have loved them; we have been very close. However I happen to be able to testify that there is evil in the church. That is why leaven is included in this offering. This speaks of the visible church down on earth, the church as you and I see it and know it. There is evil in it. The Lord knew that long before the church even existed!

> **And ye shall offer with the bread seven lambs without blemish of the first year, and one young bullock, and two rams: they shall be for a burnt offering unto the LORD, with their meat offering, and their drink offerings, even an offering made by fire, of sweet savour unto the LORD.**

> Then ye shall sacrifice one kid of the goats for a sin of-
> fering, and two lambs of the first year for a sacrifice of
> peace offerings.
>
> And the priest shall wave them with the bread of the
> firstfruits for a wave offering before the LORD, with the
> two lambs: they shall be holy to the LORD for the priest
> [Lev. 23:18–20].

All the offerings are to be made at this time. All that Christ is and all
that He has done have been made over to the church. Believers can
draw upon Him for everything. You can come to Him for salvation,
first of all. You can come to Him for help and for mercy, for sympathy
and for comfort. You can come to Him in all the situations of life. All
the offerings were made at this time.

Isn't it interesting how the Lord, in these pictures, is giving to you
and me some of the greatest truths? He uses pictures rather than cold,
theological terms.

> And ye shall proclaim on the selfsame day, that it may
> be an holy convocation unto you: ye shall do no servile
> work therein: it shall be a statute for ever in all your
> dwellings throughout your generations [Lev. 23:21].

They were to rest on that day and cease from their own works. That is
what you and I are to do when we come to Christ. "Not by works of
righteousness which we have done, but according to his mercy he
saved us, by the washing of regeneration, and renewing of the Holy
Ghost" (Titus 3:5).

> And when ye reap the harvest of your land, thou shalt
> not make clean riddance of the corners of thy field when
> thou reapest, neither shall thou gather any gleaning of
> thy harvest: thou shalt leave them unto the poor, and to
> the stranger: I am the LORD your God [Lev. 23:22].

The holy day was adapted to the land. In the midst of the celebration they were to remember the poor and the stranger.

That is the practical side of the work of the church and of all believers today. We have been saved by grace, but we should attempt to get the Word of God out to folk and be helpful to them. I do not believe the church has any right to engage in any social service in which they do not present the gospel. We are to feed people and reach out to them in their need, but along with this we must present the gospel to them. We should remember that a man with an empty stomach is not going to be very eager to listen to the gospel. James has some things to say about that (James 2:14–20).

This also looks forward to the great harvest at the end of the age, after the rapture of the church, when God will remember the Gentiles. James 1:18 says, "Of his own will begat he us with the word of truth, that we should be a kind of firstfruits of his creatures." The early church was Jewish and was firstfruits, but it was to be followed by a great company of Gentiles. Our Lord tells about the end of the age: "The field is the world; the good seed are the children of the kingdom; but the tares are the children of the wicked one; the enemy that sowed them is the devil; the harvest is the end of the world; and the reapers are the angels" (Matt. 13:38–39). This is the judgment at the end of the age. Angels are not connected in any way to the Rapture. This is the judgment that is coming that is in mind here. "Behold my servant, whom I uphold; mine elect, in whom my soul delighteth; I have put my spirit upon him: he shall bring forth judgment to the Gentiles" (Isa. 42:1).

THE HOLY SEASON OF TRUMPETS

And the LORD spake unto Moses, saying,

Speak unto the children of Israel, saying, In the seventh month, in the first day of the month, shall ye have a sabbath, a memorial of blowing of trumpets, an holy convocation.

Ye shall do no servile work therein; but ye shall offer an offering made by fire unto the LORD [Lev. 23:23–25].

The date here is important. Three feasts take place in the seventh month. It is sort of a sabbatic month, just as there is a sabbatic day and a sabbatic year. This marked the beginning of the civil year as Passover marked the beginning of the religious year.

The blowing of two silver trumpets was used in moving Israel through the wilderness (Num. 10). The trumpets were blown seven times to get them on the march. There are seven trumpets in the Revelation which cover the Great Tribulation period and which will see Israel restored to the land for the Kingdom Age. "And it shall come to pass in that day, that the great trumpet shall be blown, and they shall come which were ready to perish in the land of Assyria, and the outcasts in the land of Egypt, and shall worship the LORD in the holy mount at Jerusalem" (Isa. 27:13). "And he shall send his angels with a great sound of a trumpet, and they shall gather together his elect from the four winds, from one end of heaven to the other" (Matt. 24:31).

Before the restoration of Israel the church will have left the earth already. They will hear the voice of the Lord like a trumpet. These are now the people left on earth who will hear the sound of the trumpet.

"Blessed is the people that know the joyful sound: they shall walk, O LORD, in the light of thy countenance" (Ps. 89:15).

The trumpets are connected with the coming judgment.

THE HOLY SEASON OF THE
GREAT DAY OF ATONEMENT

And the LORD spake unto Moses, saying,

Also on the tenth day of this seventh month there shall be a day of atonement: it shall be an holy convocation unto you; and ye shall afflict your souls, and offer an offering made by fire unto the LORD.

And ye shall do no work in that same day: for it is a day of atonement, to make an atonement for you before the LORD your God.

For whatsoever soul it be that shall not be afflicted in that same day, he shall be cut off from among his people.

And whatsoever soul it be that doeth any work in that same day, the same soul will I destroy from among his people.

Ye shall do no manner of work: it shall be a statute for ever throughout your generations in all your dwellings.

It shall be unto you a sabbath of rest, and ye shall afflict your souls: in the ninth day of the month at even, from even unto even, shall ye celebrate your sabbath [Lev. 23:26–32].

The great Day of Atonement was fully covered in chapter 16. Three times Scripture says, "Ye shall afflict your souls." It was a solemn day rather than a feast day, which was different from all the others.

In contrast to this, it is interesting to note that the trumpet of Jubilee was sounded every fifty years on the Day of Atonement, and that it denoted joy and rejoicing (Lev. 25:8–9). There is deliverance when the price is paid for your salvation and mine. That is the year of Jubilee. What a glorious year that must have been!

THE HOLY SEASON OF TABERNACLES

And the LORD spake unto Moses, saying,

Speak unto the children of Israel, saying, The fifteenth day of this seventh month shall be the feast of tabernacles for seven days unto the LORD.

On the first day shall be an holy convocation: ye shall do no servile work therein.

Seven days ye shall offer an offering made by fire unto the LORD: on the eighth day shall be an holy convocation unto you; and ye shall offer an offering made by fire unto the LORD: it is a solemn assembly; and ye shall do no servile work therein [Lev. 23:33–36].

This is the third feast in the seventh month. It was both a memorial and a prophetic holy season. It followed the great Day of Atonement by only a few days. As a memorial, it spoke of their days of wandering in the wilderness when they dwelt in booths. It points prophetically to the time when God will have fully removed their sin, and they will dwell again safely in the Promised Land. "And I will pour upon the house of David, and upon the inhabitants of Jerusalem, the spirit of grace and of supplications: and they shall look upon me whom they have pierced, and they shall mourn for him, as one mourneth for his only son, and shall be in bitterness for him, as one that is in bitterness for his firstborn" (Zech. 12:10). "In that day there shall be a fountain opened to the house of David and to the inhabitants of Jerusalem for sin and for uncleanness" (Zech. 13:1). "But they shall sit every man under his vine and under his fig tree; and none shall make them afraid: for the mouth of the LORD of hosts hath spoken it" (Mic. 4:4).

These are the feasts of the LORD, which ye shall proclaim to be holy convocations, to offer an offering made by fire unto the LORD, a burnt offering, and a meat offering, a sacrifice, and drink offerings, every thing upon his day:

Beside the sabbaths of the LORD, and beside your gifts, and beside all your vows, and beside all your freewill offerings, which ye give unto the LORD [Lev. 23:37–38].

This is a special emphasis on the feast days to revel in what God delights for the benefit of His people.

Also in the fifteenth day of the seventh month, when ye have gathered in the fruit of the land, ye shall keep a

feast unto the LORD seven days: on the first day shall be a sabbath, and on the eighth day shall be a sabbath.

And ye shall take you on the first day the boughs of goodly trees, branches of palm trees, and the boughs of thick trees, and willows of the brook; and ye shall rejoice before the LORD your God seven days.

And ye shall keep it a feast unto the LORD seven days in the year. It shall be a statute for ever in your generations: ye shall celebrate it in the seventh month.

Ye shall dwell in booths seven days: all that are Israelites born shall dwell in booths:

That your generations may know that I made the children of Israel to dwell in booths, when I brought them out of the land of Egypt: I am the LORD your God.

And Moses declared unto the children of Israel the feasts of the LORD [Lev. 23:39-44].

After the great Day of Atonement when there was made a full expiation of their sins, and the harvest and fruit of the land were gathered in, there was observed this very joyful occasion. They were to dwell in booths to remind them of the wilderness wanderings, but also to point them to the future. Hebrews 11 tells us that they all died in faith, not having received the promises, but having seen them afar off. They were persuaded of them and they embraced them. They were looking forward to that day when they would not dwell in booths as in the wilderness, but they would be in the millennial age. That is the hope for this earth.

This holy season will be observed during the Millennium: "And it shall come to pass, that every one that is left of all the nations which came against Jerusalem shall even go up from year to year to worship the King, the LORD of hosts, and to keep the feast of tabernacles. And it shall be, that whoso will not come up of all the families of the earth unto Jerusalem to worship the King, the LORD of hosts, even upon them shall be no rain. And if the family of Egypt go not up, and come not, that have no rain; there shall be the plague, wherewith the LORD will smite the heathen that come not up to keep the feast of tabernacles" (Zech. 14:16–18). You will find it interesting to read that whole chapter of Zechariah 14.

This feast is not only prophetic of the Millennium, but also points to eternity and the everlasting Kingdom. "And I heard a great voice out of heaven saying, Behold, the tabernacle of God is with men, and he will dwell with them, and they shall be his people, and God himself shall be with them, and be their God" (Rev. 21:3). This is the fulfillment of the great Feast of Tabernacles. For seven days in the seventh month they were to rejoice. This speaks of the final and full rejoicing of God's earthly people. (His heavenly people will be with Him in the New Jerusalem.) Friends, there is a great future ahead for us!

CHAPTER 24

THEME: Olive oil for the golden lampstand; fine flour for the table of showbread; death penalty for the sin of blasphemy

This chapter seems to be out of place with what has gone before. The items in this chapter seem to be disconnected. The oil for the lampstand and the bread for the table do not seem to belong between the Feast of Tabernacles and the Sabbatic year. Nevertheless, this is the method the Holy Spirit uses on another occasion. In Numbers 8:1–4 there are the instructions for lighting the lights, and a brief description is inserted between the gifts of the princes and the cleansing of the Levites. I think it teaches that all is to be done in the light and leading of the Holy Spirit. The same lesson is to be drawn here. The celebration of the feasts and the observances of the Sabbatic and Jubilee years must be performed in the light of the Holy Spirit and in the strength and power of Christ. That is very important.

There are some practical implications which must not be overlooked. The people were to furnish the oil for the lampstand and the fine flour for the bread on the table. God made them participants in the provision and worship of the tabernacle. God, by some miracle, could have furnished the oil and the flour and the workmanship for the table and the lampstand. However, He wanted the people to participate.

That is the way I feel about getting out the Word of God. In every local congregation there are ways for you to get involved in the work of the Lord. Just keep your eyes open and you will notice something to do. I remember when I was teaching a little Bible study to a Boy Scout troop. I doubt whether any one of those boys ever did a good deed—they almost put me in the hospital! I really had to be stern with them. A couple of men from the church came in one night and saw what a problem I had with those boys. So they volunteered their help. It was wonderful to have them sit with the boys while I taught the Bible study.

All those who love the Word of God should get involved in getting the message to people. God says, "You bring the oil; you bring the flour."

The importance of the lampstand cannot be overlooked. It was probably the most accurate and beautiful picture of Christ in all the tabernacle. It was solid gold and beautifully wrought into seven branches of almond boughs from one main stem.

Aaron had sole charge of the lights of the lampstand to keep them burning (Exod. 30:7–8). It is important to see that today the lamps are in the hands of our Great High Priest. Jesus Christ has said that He is the Light of the world. Before He left, He told His own that they were to be the light of the world. Paul uses this same idea when he says, ". . . among whom ye shine as lights in the world" (Phil. 2:15). In Revelation 1 and 2, the Lord Jesus Christ as our Great High Priest walks in the midst of the lampstands today to keep us shining. He pours in the oil which is the filling with the Holy Spirit. He trims the wicks so that the light will burn brighter. He removes the light when it refuses to burn—this is the sin unto death which John mentions in his epistle.

Therefore the insertion of the lampstand and the showbread in this section is not out of place.

The second incident in the Book of Leviticus is found in this chapter: the son of an Israelitish mother and an Egyptian father blasphemed. This is another example of the problem and difficulty presented by the mixed multitude that came out of Egypt with Israel. They were problem children and troublemakers. They correspond to those in the church today who are torn between the world on one hand and serving God on the other.

OLIVE OIL FOR THE GOLDEN LAMPSTAND

And the LORD spake unto Moses, saying,

Command the children of Israel, that they bring unto thee pure oil olive beaten for the light, to cause the lamps to burn continually [Lev. 24:1–2].

The people of Israel were to furnish the olive oil, and since the seven lamps burned continually, both day and night, this was no small item. This gave each Israelite, as well as the tribe of Levi, an interest in the service of the tabernacle. The olive oil was to be pure, free from leaves and all impurities. It was not to be pressed out, but beaten out, to produce the very finest grade. The best was to be used, for the oil speaks of the Holy Spirit.

> **Without the vail of the testimony, in the tabernacle of the congregation, shall Aaron order it from the evening unto the morning before the LORD continually: it shall be a statute for ever in your generations.**

> **He shall order the lamps upon the pure candlestick before the LORD continually [Lev. 24:3–4].**

The lamps were to be kept lit continually while the tabernacle was set up. (Obviously, when they marched in the wilderness, they did not hold up lighted candlesticks.) And we note that Aaron alone controlled the use and the service of the lampstand. "And Aaron shall burn thereon sweet incense every morning: when he dresseth the lamps, he shall burn incense upon it. And when Aaron lighteth the lamps at even, he shall burn incense upon it, a perpetual incense before the LORD throughout your generations" (Exod. 30:7–8).

The Lord Jesus Christ is walking in the midst of the lampstands today. He is our Great High Priest. He trims them every now and then as He moves into our hearts and lives. Sometimes He must snuff out a light that is giving off smoke instead of light.

FINE FLOUR FOR THE TABLE OF SHOWBREAD

> **And thou shalt take fine flour, and bake twelve cakes thereof: two tenth deals shall be in one cake.**

> **And thou shalt set them in two rows, six on a row, upon the pure table before the LORD.**

> **And thou shalt put pure frankincense upon each row,
> that it may be on the bread for a memorial even an offer-
> ing made by fire unto the LORD [Lev. 24:5-7].**

The fine flour was to be furnished by the people, as was the olive oil.
As the oil speaks of the Holy Spirit, so the bread speaks of Christ.
"And Jesus said unto them, I am the bread of life: he that cometh to me
shall never hunger; and he that believeth on me shall never thirst"
(John 6:35).

Fine flour means it was of wheat. The frankincense was a natural
gum to be a gift from the people. The bread speaks of Christ, and the
frankincense speaks of the wonderful fragrance of His humanity.

> **Every sabbath he shall set it in order before the LORD
> continually, being taken from the children of Israel by
> an everlasting covenant.**

> **And it shall be Aaron's and his sons'; and they shall eat
> it in the holy place: for it is most holy unto him of the
> offerings of the LORD made by fire by a perpetual statute
> [Lev. 24:8-9].**

The bread would stay on the table for a week. It was to be changed on
the Sabbath, and the old bread was to be eaten by Aaron and his
sons—and always in the Holy Place. When David and his men were in
desperate need, Ahimelech gave him some of the showbread to eat
(1 Sam. 21:4-6). Our Lord calls attention to this when they criticized
His disciples for eating grain on the Sabbath Day (Matt. 12:3-4).

The bread and the light speak of Christ. "I am the living bread
which came down from heaven: if any man eat of this bread, he shall
live for ever: and the bread that I will give is my flesh, which I will
give for the life of the world" (John 6:51). "Then spake Jesus again
unto them, saying, I am the light of the world: he that followeth me
shall not walk in darkness, but shall have the light of life" (John 8:12).

We must feed on Him if we are to serve Him. And anything we do
for Him must be done in His light through the Holy Spirit.

DEATH PENALTY FOR THE SIN OF BLASPHEMY

There are only two incidents or episodes recorded in the Book of Leviticus. One is the incident of Nadab and Abihu back in Leviticus 10, and now we come to this incident. It seems entirely out of keeping with the instructions given here, but we need to recognize the fact that God is teaching a great lesson concerning blasphemy.

And the son of an Israelitish woman, whose father was an Egyptian, went out among the children of Israel: and this son of the Israelitish woman and a man of Israel strove together in the camp;

And the Israelitish woman's son blasphemed the name of the LORD, and cursed. And they brought him unto Moses: (and his mother's name was Shelomith, the daughter of Dibri, of the tribe of Dan:)

And they put him in ward, that the mind of the LORD might be shewed them [Lev. 24:10–12].

This boy who did the blaspheming is of a mixed race—his mother was of the tribe of Dan and his father was an Egyptian. There was a mixed multitude that went out of Egypt along with the children of Israel (Exod. 12:38). We are going to see that this group started trouble in the camp; they would murmur and cause strife. "And the mixed multitude that was among them fell a-lusting: and the children of Israel also wept again, and said, Who shall give us flesh to eat?" (Num. 11:4).

We can see why these would be problem children, troublemakers. When the day came for the children of Israel to leave the land of Egypt and go out into the Promised Land, the Egyptian father would stay in Egypt and the Israelitish mother would go. There is a separation right there.

This is one of the reasons that God told His people then (and He tells us now) that there should not be intermarriage between a believer and an unbeliever. This does not have anything to do with race. It is wrong for a believer to marry an unbeliever regardless of the color of the skin. Even though both are the same color, it is still wrong for a believer to marry an unbeliever. *God* says that. I would never have known it is wrong if God hadn't said it.

This boy has a problem. He must make a decision whether to go the way of the father or the way of the mother. The problem is that the decision is never really made. Sure, he made an initial decision, but then in his mind the question would always reappear, *I wonder if I should have done the other thing and stayed with Dad.* This mixed multitude has an eternal question mark before them. It was a hard decision to leave Egypt in the first place. Then their thoughts constantly go back to Egypt, and when the going gets rough, they are the first to complain.

Now, friends, we have those same people in the church today. There is the unsaved person in the church who wants one foot in the church, but he has the other foot out in the world. They are the troublemakers. It has always made me wonder whether the troublemaker is really a saved person. I cannot understand a really born-again believer in the Lord Jesus Christ trying to block the giving out of the Word of God. The greatest opposition I have had to my radio broadcast that gives out the Word of God has not come from those outside the church; it has been the church members who have tried to wreck this radio program. I was never so shocked in my life. One would expect them to say, "Brother, God bless you. I hope you can get the Word of God out to people." No, my friend, they didn't want to have any part in it.

Now this boy got into a fight. We can easily understand how that could come about. He did not have a place in the tribe of Dan, but was a hanger-on who had access to the camp of Israel. After he got into the fight, he blasphemed the name of God. He cursed the name of the Lord, that name which was so sacred in Israel that it was not even voiced. It evidently was the Hebrew tetragrammaton YHWH. There is even a question today about how to pronounce the name of the Lord. Is it Jehovah or Jahweh? The name is so holy that the Israelites did not even pronounce it, but this blasphemer could pronounce it!

I was invited to a private club by one of the members, and we had lunch there. A man at the table next to us used the name of God more than I have ever used it in any sermon. But He didn't use it like I use it in a sermon! He was blaspheming. And God feels no differently about him than He did about this boy in Leviticus.

And the LORD spake unto Moses, saying,

Bring forth him that hath cursed without the camp; and let all that heard him lay their hands upon his head, and let all the congregation stone him.

And thou shalt speak unto the children of Israel, saying, Whosoever curseth his God shall bear his sin.

And he that blasphemeth the name of the LORD, he shall surely be put to death, and all the congregation shall certainly stone him: as well the stranger, as he that is born in the land, when he blasphemeth the name of the LORD, shall be put to death [Lev. 24:13–16].

God handed down His verdict of guilty, and the penalty was death by stoning. The seriousness of the crime is measured by the penalty which God inflicted. All who heard the blasphemy must place their hands on his head, denoting a placing of guilt solely on the young man. The death penalty is required for blaspheming God, and it is established that the penalty shall be paid by both the Israelite and the stranger.

And he that killeth any man shall surely be put to death.

And he that killeth a beast shall make it good; beast for beast.

And if a man cause a blemish in his neighbour; as he hath done, so shall it be done to him;

Breach for breach, eye for eye, tooth for tooth: as he hath caused a blemish in a man, so shall it be done to him again.

And he that killeth a beast, he shall restore it: and he that killeth a man, he shall be put to death.

Ye shall have one manner of law, as well for the stranger, as for one of your own country: for I am the LORD your God [Lev. 24:17–22].

We have developed some soft notions. The penalty for murdering a man is stated right here. War protesters like to print "Thou shalt not kill" on their banners. I am still waiting to see a banner that says "He that killeth any man shall surely be put to death."

There was established here what is known as *lex talionis,* an eye for an eye and a tooth for a tooth. This was the penalty which was inflicted literally. One law applied to both the Israelite and the stranger.

And Moses spake to the children of Israel, that they should bring forth him that had cursed out of the camp, and stone him with stones. And the children of Israel did as the LORD commanded Moses [Lev. 24:23].

There is a great moral lesson here. The name of our God is sacred and must be protected. Blasphemy is a crime of the deepest hue. Also, human life is sacred and must be protected. God provides also for the protection of personal property.

God is righteous in all His dealings. We, too, are guilty before God—"The soul that sinneth, it shall die." But Christ has borne our sentence of death. "Surely he hath borne our griefs, and carried our sorrows: yet we did esteem him stricken, smitten of God, and afflicted. But he was wounded for our transgressions, he was bruised for our iniquities: the chastisement of our peace was upon him; and with his stripes we are healed. All we like sheep have gone astray; we have turned every one to his own way; and the LORD hath laid on him the iniquity of us all" (Isa. 53:4–6).

CHAPTER 25

THEME: *The sabbatical year; the year of Jubilee; the redemption of property; the redemption of persons*

Not only was the Mosaic economy directed to the people of Israel, but it also pertained particularly to the land of Palestine. This is emphasized in this chapter. The laws given here could not be enforced until Israel entered the land of Canaan. They could not possibly be adapted to the wilderness. There is a constant and almost monotonous reference to and repetition of the word *land*—"When ye come into the land," "rest unto the land," and "proclaim liberty throughout all the land." That last phrase is found ten times. Everything in this chapter is tied down to the land which God gave Israel. The Mosaic economy was directed to a peculiar people, Israel, and to a particular land, Palestine. Furthermore, it is directed to a people engaged in agriculture.

There are those who try to saddle the Old Testament Law as a way of life upon the church. These laws don't fit in California, and they won't fit other areas of our nation. "Proclaim liberty throughout all the land" is inscribed on our Liberty Bell in Philadelphia. Yet, we need always remember that these laws were given to a particular people in a particular land.

One cannot read Leviticus, nor the rest of the Bible, without noticing the recurrence of the number *seven*. It is the number used to denote completeness. It does not mean perfection in every instance, but it denotes completeness. There is a definite connection of the many occurences of the number seven in Leviticus with the number seven in Revelation. Both books use it in a structural way. Time was divided into sevens both for the civil and ceremonial calendars. There is the seventh day, the seventh week, the seventh month, the seventh year. The calendar was geared to Sabbatic times and the Levitical code was run on wheels of seven cycles. This occurs again in Revelation.

God rested on the seventh day, not because He was tired, but because He had completed creation in six days, and there was no more to do. The Sabbath was made the basic unit of measurement of time, and then from the Sabbath there were ever-expanding units of time measurement.

THE SABBATICAL YEAR

And the Lord spake unto Moses in mount Sinai, saying [Lev. 25:1].

It should be noted that this reverts back to Mount Sinai, but it is to be put into effect when they get into the Land. Remember that God spoke out of the tabernacle in Leviticus 1:1.

Speak unto the children of Israel, and say unto them, When ye come into the land which I give you, then shall the land keep a sabbath unto the Lord [Lev. 25:2].

This is amazing. There is a sabbath for the land as well as for man. The seventh day is for man, and the seventh year is for the land.

The seventh day hearkens back to creation when God rested from His labors, for His work of creation was complete. *Sabbath* means rest, and in its ultimate meaning it refers to the rest of redemption. "There remaineth therefore a rest to the people of God. For he that is entered into his rest, he also hath ceased from his own works, as God did from his. Let us labour therefore to enter into that rest, lest any man fall after the same example of unbelief" (Heb. 4:9–11). *Rest* in these verses means literally "keeping of a sabbath."

It is obvious in this day of scientific agriculture that letting the land lie fallow on the seventh year was good for the land. It was also a rest for those who tilled the soil, although they could discharge other necessary duties. This Sabbatical year for the land was to deliver the Israelite from covetousness. Actually, it was the breaking of this regulation concerning the Sabbatical year that sent Israel into the seventy years Babylonian captivity (2 Chron. 36:21). They failed to keep seventy Sabbatic years over a period of 490 years; so they went into captivity for seventy years.

> **Six years thou shalt sow thy field, and six years thou shalt prune thy vineyard, and gather in the fruit thereof;**
>
> **But in the seventh year shall be a sabbath of rest unto the land, a sabbath for the LORD: thou shalt neither sow thy field, nor prune thy vineyard [Lev. 25:3–4].**

This makes it perfectly clear that the Sabbatical year related to the land. They were to sow their fields and prune their vineyards for six years, and then neither sow nor prune on the seventh year. There is a curse upon the earth as well as upon man, and it is by the sweat of man's brow that he extracts bread from the soil. There will be a day when the curse shall be lifted from creation (Rom. 8:20–22 and Isa. 35:1–2).

The southland where I was reared has learned, to its sorrow, that one should let the land lie fallow. A great deal of the land has been worn out by planting cotton every year, year after year. The Sabbatical year was actually a good agricultural principle which God gave to them. It is quite interesting that God knows all about farming, isn't it?

> **That which groweth of its own accord of thy harvest thou shalt not reap, neither gather the grapes of thy vine undressed: for it is a year of rest unto the land.**
>
> **And the sabbath of the land shall be meat for you; for thee, and for thy servant, and for thy maid, and for thy hired servant, and for thy stranger that sojourneth with thee,**
>
> **And for thy cattle, and for the beast that are in thy land, shall all the increase thereof be meat [Lev. 25:5–7].**

This shows how the physical needs of the people were supplied during the Sabbatical year. The land was so productive that it was not

necessary to plant each year. In the Euphrates Valley, in the days of
Abraham, it was not necessary to plant at all. The grain grew without
planting. The ground in Israel produced enough to supply the needs
of the owner, his servants, and the stranger. Even the cattle could sur-
vive and probably grew fat by grazing on the untilled land. God took
care of both man and beast, Israelite and stranger, rich and poor during the year of rest. They were all given enough to eat. However, they
could not harvest anything to market it.

Years ago, before all the subdivisions were built, there were many
fine vineyards near Pasadena. I had a very fine neighbor who had a
wonderful vineyard of Concord grapes. He was a generous man and he
would always bring me a basket or two during the season. He was a
Seventh Day Adventist and at times he would try to goad me about the
Sabbath Day. He would ask me why I didn't keep the Sabbath Day. I
would tell him that I did keep the Sabbath Day—on Saturday and on
Sunday and on Monday and on Tuesday and every day of the week. I
tried to explain to him that *sabbath* means rest and that we have entered into the rest of redemption. We have ceased from works and put
our trust in Jesus Christ which makes every day a day of rest, a rest in
Jesus Christ. Of course, he didn't like it that way. Then I would ask
him a question. "Are you keeping the Mosaic Law? Are you keeping
the Sabbath as they did in Israel?" He assured me that he was. Then I
showed him chapter 25 of Leviticus. I told him there was not a Sabbath Day only, but there was also a Sabbatical year. In that year the
poor people could go into the vineyard and glean grapes. I asked him
to let me know when he would observe that Sabbatical year so I could
get my basket and glean some of his grapes. He answered, "You'd
better not go into that vineyard without my permission!" May I say to
you, he was not keeping the Mosaic Law. He was keeping only a small
part of it. He did not keep the Sabbatical year nor the year of Jubilee.

God was teaching Israel several lessons. He never permitted any
one of them to monopolize the land so that the poor people were not
taken care of. God was protecting the land and the poor people at the
same time. Also He was teaching them that the land was cursed but
that the time would come when the land would produce in abun-
dance.

Today, people worry about the population explosion and the inability of the earth to produce enough food for the people. When the curse is removed, my friend, this earth will produce in a way never seen since the fall of man. God is the supplier of all human needs. God is the owner of this earth.

THE YEAR OF JUBILEE

And thou shalt number seven sabbaths of years unto thee, seven times seven years; and the space of the seven sabbaths of years shall be unto thee forty and nine years [Lev. 25:8].

This continues in the multiples of seven. Seven Sabbatical years were numbered and this made forty-nine years. Then, the following year, the fiftieth, was set aside as the year of Jubilee. The year of Jubilee was a continuing of the number seven to the ever-ascending scale of the calendar. It was the largest unit of time—fifty years.

Today we operate by leases. People may have a fifty-year lease or a ninety-nine-year lease. God worked on that basis, also. There were two years of Jubilee in every century.

Then shalt thou cause the trumpet of the jubile to sound on the tenth day of the seventh month, in the day of atonement shall ye make the trumpet sound throughout all your land [Lev. 25:9].

This was the crowning point of the entire sabbatical structure of the nation. It was the *SHeNATH HAYOBHEL,* the year of Jubilee. In many respects it was the most anticipated and joyful period of the Mosaic economy. The *KEREN HAYOBHEL* meant the horn of a ram, and in the time the *YOBHEL* came to mean trumpet. It is translated twenty-one times as "jubilee," five times as "ram's horn," and once as "trumpet."

After Israel was settled in the land, it is difficult to see how one blast of the trumpet could be heard from Dan to Beersheba. It is reasonable to conclude that in every populated area there was a simultaneous blowing of the ram's horn to usher in the year of Jubilee. I think it would begin at the tabernacle or temple. There would be a person stationed far enough away to be able to hear it, and then the trumpet note would be passed on and on out to the very end of the land.

> **And ye shall hallow the fiftieth year, and proclaim liberty throughout all the land unto all the inhabitants thereof: it shall be a jubile unto you; and ye shall return every man unto his possession, and ye shall return every man unto his family [Lev. 25:10].**

In that day people could mortgage their land, but in the year of Jubilee that land would return back to the original owner. This was the way God protected the land from leaving the original owner. The land could be taken away for a period of fifty years, but in the year of Jubilee the land went back to the original owner or to his descendants.

If a man had sold himself into slavery, when that trumpet was sounded he went free. The shackles were broken.

This is how we are freed today. The Greek word for trumpet is *kerux* and the verb *kerusso* means to proclaim or to herald. The year of Jubilee is likened to this age of grace when the gospel is preached to slaves of sin and captives of Satan. "But God be thanked, that ye were the servants of sin, but ye have obeyed from the heart that form of doctrine which was delivered you. Being then made free from sin, ye became the servants of righteousness. For the wages of sin is death; but the gift of God is eternal life through Jesus Christ our Lord" (Rom. 6:17–18, 23). The Lord Jesus Christ said, "And ye shall know the truth, and the truth shall make you free. . . . If the Son therefore shall make you free, ye shall be free indeed" (John 8:32, 36).

In the year of Jubilee everything went free. All mortgages were canceled. When you come to Jesus Christ, my friend, the sin question is settled. He paid the penalty. It is all settled, and you go free. He makes you free! "But now being made free from sin, and become servants to God, ye have your fruit unto holiness, and the end everlasting life" (Rom. 6:22). "Stand fast therefore in the liberty wherewith Christ hath made us free, and be not entangled again with the yoke of bondage" (Gal. 5:1).

In this connection it is interesting to note the words of our Lord in the synagogue at Nazareth: "And there was delivered unto him the book of the prophet Esaias. And when he had opened the book, he found the place where it was written, The Spirit of the Lord is upon me, because he hath anointed me to preach the gospel to the poor; he hath sent me to heal the brokenhearted, to preach deliverance to the captives, and recovering of sight to the blind, to set at liberty them that are bruised, To preach the acceptable year of the Lord. And he closed the book, and he gave it again to the minister, and sat down. And the eyes of all them that were in the synagogue were fastened on him. And he began to say unto them, This day is this scripture fulfilled in your ears" (Luke 4:17–21).

"To preach the gospel to the poor" is to herald it, to trumpet it. Isn't this the year of Jubilee—to heal the brokenhearted, to preach deliverance to the captives, to set at liberty them that are bruised?

Possibly the best application and final fulfillment of the year of Jubilee will be in the Millennium as it relates directly to the nation Israel. I would encourage you to read Isaiah 11, 35, and 40, Jeremiah 23, Micah 4, and Revelation 20.

> **A jubile, shall that fiftieth year be unto you: ye shall not sow, neither reap that which groweth of itself in it, nor gather the grapes in it of thy vine undressed.**

> **For it is the jubile; it shall be holy unto you: ye shall eat the increase thereof out of the field [Lev. 25:11–12].**

The year of Jubilee followed a Sabbatical year when the land lay fallow. God promised to provide providentially for them. They were to obey. God would provide.

> **In the year of this jubile ye shall return every man unto his possession.**

> **And if thou sell ought unto thy neighbour, or buyest ought of thy neighbour's hand, ye shall not oppress one another:**

According to the number of years after the jubile thou shalt buy of thy neighbour, and according unto the number of years of the fruits he shall sell unto thee:

According to the multitude of years thou shalt increase the price thereof, and according to the fewness of years thou shalt diminish the price of it: for according to the number of the years of the fruits doth he sell unto thee.

Ye shall not therefore oppress one another; but thou shalt fear thy God: for I am the LORD your God.

Wherefore ye shall do my statutes, and keep my judgments, and do them; and ye shall dwell in the land in safety.

And the land shall yield her fruit, and ye shall eat your fill, and dwell therein in safety.

And if ye shall say, What shall we eat the seventh year? behold, we shall not sow, nor gather in our increase:

Then I will command my blessing upon you in the sixth year, and it shall bring forth fruit for three years.

And ye shall sow the eighth year, and eat yet of old fruit until the ninth year; until her fruits come in ye shall eat of the old store.

The land shall not be sold for ever: for the land is mine; for ye are strangers and sojourners with me.

And in all the land of your possession ye shall grant a redemption for the land [Lev. 25:13–24].

This section explains that all property and possessions were to be returned to the original owner. This prevented any one individual or group from getting possession of most of the land while the rest became extremely poor. It preserved a balance in Israel. This was not a choice between communism and capitalism, but it was God's plan. He retained ownership of the land and Israel held it in perpetuity.

God promised His blessing upon them. He promised to bless the land in the sixth year. They would sow again on the eighth year and they would eat of the old fruit of the land until the ninth year when it would produce again. God makes it very clear to them in verse 23: "The land shall not be sold for ever: for the land is mine."

THE REDEMPTION OF PROPERTY

If thy brother be waxen poor, and hath sold away some of his possessions, and if any of his kin come to redeem it, then shall he redeem that which his brother sold.

And if the man have none to redeem it, and himself be able to redeem it;

Then let him count the years of the sale thereof, and restore the overplus unto the man to whom he sold it; that he may return unto his possession [Lev. 25:25–27].

It was a long time from one year of Jubilee to the next. If a man lost his property shortly after a Jubilee, there was the possibility he would not be alive to enjoy it the next time a year of Jubilee came around. So God made another provision for the recovery of the land. If there was a rich relative, he was able to redeem the property if he was willing to do so, and then the land could be restored to the original owner. It depended on the willingness of the kinsman. This is the law of the kinsman-redeemer which we will see in operation in the Book of Ruth.

But if he be not able to restore it to him, then that which is sold shall remain in the hand of him that hath bought it until the year of jubile: and in the jubile it shall go out, and he shall return unto his possession.

And if a man sell a dwelling house in a walled city, then he may redeem it within a whole year after it is sold; within a full year may he redeem it.

And if it be not redeemed within the space of a full year, then the house that is in the walled city shall be established for ever to him that bought it throughout his generations: it shall not go out in the jubile.

But the houses of the villages which have no wall round about them shall be counted as the fields of the country: they may be redeemed, and they shall go out in the jubile.

Notwithstanding the cities of the Levites, and the houses of the cities of their possession, may the Levites redeem at any time.

And if a man purchase of the Levites, then the house that was sold, and the city of his possession, shall go out in the year of jubile: for the houses of the cities of the Levites are their possession among the children of Israel.

But the field of the suburbs of their cities may not be sold; for it is their perpetual possession [Lev. 25:28–34].

Laws were also made concerning dwellings and buildings on property. Depreciation was taken into consideration. There were different rules applying to the Levites.

THE REDEMPTION OF PERSONS

And if thy brother be waxen poor, and fallen in decay with thee; then thou shalt relieve him: yea, though he be a stranger, or a sojourner; that he may live with thee.

Take thou no usury of him, or increase: but fear thy God; that thy brother may live with thee.

Thou shalt not give him thy money upon usury, nor lend him thy victuals for increase [Lev. 25:35–37].

God was explicit about the care of unfortunate folk. They were to be helped; they were not to be taken advantage of.

> I am the LORD your God, which brought you forth out of the land of Egypt, to give you the land of Canaan, and to be your God.
>
> And if thy brother that dwelleth by thee be waxen poor, and be sold unto thee; thou shalt not compel him to serve as a bondservant:
>
> But as an hired servant, and as a sojourner, he shall be with thee, and shall serve thee unto the year of jubile:
>
> And then shall he depart from thee, both he and his children with him, and shall return unto his own family, and unto the possession of his fathers shall he return.
>
> For they are my servants, which I brought forth out of the land of Egypt: they shall not be sold as bondsmen.
>
> Thou shalt not rule over him with rigour, but shalt fear thy God.
>
> Both thy bondmen, and thy bondmaids, which thou shalt have, shall be of the heathen that are round about you; of them shall ye buy bondmen and bondmaids.
>
> Moreover, of the children of the strangers that do sojourn among you, of them shall ye buy, and of their families that are with you, which they begat in your land: and they shall be your possession.
>
> And ye shall take them as an inheritance for your children after you, to inherit them for a possession; they shall be your bondmen for ever: but over your brethren the children of Israel, ye shall not rule one over another with rigour [Lev. 25:38–46].

The poor brother who probably had a low I.Q. was to be protected from becoming a slave. He was to be treated as a hired servant, not as a slave. They were permitted to have only foreigners as slaves—which was a great step forward in a world of slavery. It is the adaptation of the Mosaic Law to the mores of that day.

And if a sojourner or stranger wax rich by thee, and thy brother that dwelleth by him wax poor, and sell himself unto the stranger or sojourner by thee, or to the stock of the stranger's family:

After that he is sold he may be redeemed again; one of his brethren may redeem him:

Either his uncle, or his uncle's son, may redeem him, or any that is nigh of kin unto him of his family may redeem him; or if he be able, he may redeem himself.

And he shall reckon with him that bought him from the year that he was sold to him unto the year of jubile: and the price of his sale shall be according unto the number of years, according to the time of a hired servant shall it be with him.

If there be yet many years behind, according unto them he shall give again the price of his redemption out of the money that he was bought for.

And if there remain but few years unto the year of jubile, then he shall count with him, and according unto his years shall he give him again the price of his redemption.

And as a yearly hired servant shall he be with him: and the other shall not rule with rigour over him in thy sight.

And if he be not redeemed in these years, then he shall go out in the year of jubile, both he, and his children with him.

> For unto me the children of Israel are servants; they are
> my servants whom I brought forth out of the land of
> Egypt: I am the LORD your God [Lev. 25:47–55].

This is the application of the law of Jubilee to the person (see verse 10) who not only had lost his property, but had to sell his person as well. He could have the services of a kinsman-redeemer if there was one who was willing and able to deliver him before the year of Jubilee.

You and I have a Kinsman-Redeemer. He is rich. Yet, for our sakes He was willing to become poor so that He might shed His precious blood to redeem us. He has redeemed not only our persons but He has also paid the price for this cursed earth. It too will be redeemed from the curse that is on it now. The law of the kinsman-redeemer points to our Lord Jesus Christ who is our Kinsman-Redeemer.

CHAPTER 26

THEME: Prologue to Israel's Magna Carta of the land;
promise of blessing; pronouncement of judgment;
prediction predicated on promise to patriarchs

This is a marvelous chapter. It is a prophetic history that covers
Israel's entire tenure of the Promised Land until the present hour
and gives the conditions in the future on which they will occupy the
land.

This section stands in a peculiar relationship to the remainder of
the Book of Leviticus. There are not great spiritual lessons and pictures here, but this is the direct word of Jehovah to the nation Israel
concerning their future. This is history prewritten and reveals the basis on which Israel entered the land of Canaan and their tenancy there.

This is an "iffy" chapter. "If" occurs nine times and it has to do
with the conditions on which they occupy the land. God says "I will"
twenty-four times. God will act and react according to their responses
to the "if". God gave them the land, but their occupancy of it is determined by their answer to the "if". Obedience is the ground of blessing
in the land. This chapter is not only the calendar of their history, but it
serves as the barometer of their blessings. Their presence in the land,
rainfall, and bountiful crops denote the favor of God. Their absence
from the land, famine, and drought denote the judgment of God because of their disobedience.

You and I are blessed with all spiritual blessings in the heavenlies
in Christ Jesus. However there are some "ifs" connected to that also.
God loves you and wants to shower you with His blessings. But you
can put up an umbrella of indifference, you can put up an umbrella of
sin, you can put up an umbrella of stepping out of the will of God.
When you do that, the sunshine of His love won't get through to you.
You must put down your umbrella to experience His spiritual blessings.

PROLOGUE TO ISRAEL'S MAGNA CARTA
OF THE LAND

Ye shall make you no idols nor graven image, neither rear you up a standing image, neither shall ye set up any image of stone in your land, to bow down unto it: for I am the LORD your God.

Ye shall keep my sabbaths, and reverence my sanctuary: I am the LORD [Lev. 26:1–2].

These two verses sum up the first part of the Ten Commandments, man's relationship with God. These are essential for Israel to maintain residence in the land. They are to meet these injunctions if they are to occupy that land. The land is given to them, but their enjoyment of it, their occupation of it, depends upon their obedience to God.

(1) They are to make no idols.

The Hebrew word for an idol *(elilim)* means a "nothing." They shall make no *nothings*. It's pretty hard to make a *nothing*, friends, and yet there are a great many folk who make a *nothing* of their relationship to God. Anything that takes the place of God is a *nothing*.

The word given for graven images means a carved wooden image. And the word for the image of stone means sculptured stone idols. The people were not to worship an image, nor even worship before an image. This is a repetition of what had already been told the people back in Leviticus 19:30.

(2) Keep the Sabbaths.

(3) Reverence the Sanctuary.

The Sabbath, the Sanctuary, and this matter of worshiping God, all come in one package. The character of Jehovah is the basis for obeying these injunctions. "I am the Lord."

PROMISE OF BLESSING

If ye walk in my statutes, and keep my commandments, and do them;

> Then I will give you rain in due season, and the land shall yield her increase, and the trees of the field shall yield their fruit.
>
> And your threshing shall reach unto the vintage, and the vintage shall reach unto the sowing time: and ye shall eat your bread to the full, and dwell in your land safely.
>
> And I will give peace in the land, and ye shall lie down, and none shall make you afraid: and I will rid evil beasts out of the land, neither shall the sword go through your land [Lev. 26:3-6].

You notice this starts with an "if". *If* they walk in the prescribed manner, then God promised these things. Their occupancy of the land is contingent upon the obedience to God's revealed will to them. God recognizes their free will. *If* you will obey, then God will bless.

It seems that in that land the primary evidence of the blessing of God in response to their obedience is rainfall. We find this repeated in Deuteronomy and in the prophets. "And I will make them and the places round about my hill a blessing; and I will cause the shower to come down in his season; there shall be showers of blessing. And the tree of the field shall yield her fruit, and the earth shall yield her increase, and they shall be safe in their land, and shall know that I am the LORD . . ." (Ezek. 34:26-27).

The prophets look forward to the day when this will be accomplished in Israel. It is a day yet to come. "Behold, the days come, saith the LORD, that the plowman shall overtake the reaper, and the treader of grapes him that soweth seed; and the mountains shall drop sweet wine, and all the hills shall melt" (Amos 9:13). "Be glad then, ye children of Zion, and rejoice in the LORD your God: for he hath given you the former rain moderately, and he will cause to come down for you the rain, the former rain, and the latter rain in the first month. And the floors shall be full of wheat, and the fats shall overflow with wine and oil" (Joel 2:23-24).

God's promise to them is the occupation of that land, showers, fruitfulness, peace. It's interesting that the little nation can't have peace today. It's no use for us to point our finger at them because the rest of us can't have peace either. It's all tied up in one little word "if". God has promised to bless *if* certain things are done.

And ye shall chase your enemies, and they shall fall before you by the sword.

And five of you shall chase an hundred, and an hundred of you shall put ten thousand to flight: and your enemies shall fall before you by the sword [Lev. 26:7–8].

Victory over their enemies would be a part of their blessing. Many times this was literally fulfilled, as you know. When they would return to God, God would raise up a Samuel, a David, a Deborah, a Gideon, or an Elijah. All these were raised up because God was making good His promise. They would be victorious over their enemies as part of their blessing. "One man of you shall chase a thousand: for the LORD your God, he it is that fighteth for you, as he hath promised you" (Josh. 23:10).

For I will have respect unto you, and make you fruitful, and multiply you, and establish my covenant with you.

And ye shall eat old store, and bring forth the old because of the new [Lev. 26:9–10].

A population explosion in Israel would be part of the blessing. Today the world doesn't think that is a blessing at all. The increase in the population would not present the problem of food shortage because the food would be so multiplied that they would have to remove the old to make room for the new.

And I will set my tabernacle among you: and my soul shall not abhor you [Lev. 26:11].

Don't tell me that God does not abhor sin. Of course He does. And He will not compromise with it in your life or my life. The tabernacle in their midst was an evident token of blessing. This is the great hope of the future which will be fulfilled finally for the eternal earth.

"And I heard a great voice out of heaven saying, Behold, the tabernacle of God is with men, and he will dwell with them, and they shall be his people, and God himself shall be with them, and be their God" (Rev. 21:3).

> **And I will walk among you, and will be your God, and ye shall be my people [Lev. 26:12].**

God promises to fellowship with those who obey Him. That is also what He tells us today. ". . . if we walk in the light, as he is in the light, we have fellowship one with another, and the blood of Jesus Christ his Son cleanseth us from all sin" (1 John 1:7). God wants to have fellowship with us. "And what agreement hath the temple of God with idols? for ye are the temple of the living God; as God hath said, I will dwell in them, and walk in them; and I will be their God, and they shall be my people" (2 Cor. 6:16).

> **I am the LORD your God, which brought you forth out of the land of Egypt, that ye should not be their bondmen; and I have broken the bands of your yoke, and made you go upright [Lev. 26:13].**

The future promise of blessing rests upon the solid history of the past when God delivered them from Egypt. He is saying to them, "I have done this for you in the past; don't you know I will do it for you in the future?" He tells us the same thing today. "Being confident of this very thing, that he which hath begun a good work in you will perform it until the day of Jesus Christ" (Phil. 1:6). You can be confident that since He has brought you up to this moment, He is going to lead you right through to the day of Jesus Christ. I'll say a *Hallelujah* to that!

PRONOUNCEMENT OF JUDGMENT

But if ye will not hearken unto me, and will not do all these commandments;

And if ye shall despise my statutes, or if your soul abhor my judgments, so that ye will not do all my commandments, but that ye break my covenant [Lev. 26:14–15].

Listen to His three "ifs" in these two verses. These are the "ifs" of a breach of the covenant: refusal to hear, refusal to do, despising and abhorring God's statutes and judgments. Breaking God's covenant would bring judgment upon the people and the land.

I also will do this unto you; I will even appoint over you terror, consumption, and the burning ague, that shall consume the eyes, and cause sorrow of heart; and ye shall sow your seed in vain, for your enemies shall eat it.

And I will set my face against you, and ye shall be slain before your enemies: they that hate you shall reign over you; and ye shall flee when none pursueth you [Lev. 26:16–17].

This is the first degree judgment—terror, consumption, burning ague, sorrow of heart, and crop failure. Their enemies will slay them, enslave them, and cause them great fear. This happened often in their sad and sordid history. We read that the anger of the Lord waxed hot against Israel, and He delivered them into the hands of spoilers who spoiled them (Jud. 2:14; 3:8; 4:2).

What the prophets did in their messages was call their attention to the fact that they had broken the covenant which God had made with them. "And they shall eat up thine harvest, and thy bread, which thy sons and thy daughters should eat . . ." (Jer. 5:17). "Thou shalt sow, but thou shalt not reap; thou shalt tread the olives, but thou shalt not anoint thee with oil; and sweet wine, but shalt not drink wine" (Mic. 6:15).

> **And if ye will not yet for all this hearken unto me, then I will punish you seven times more for your sins.**
>
> **And I will break the pride of your power; and I will make your heaven as iron, and your earth as brass:**
>
> **And your strength shall be spent in vain: for your land shall not yield her increase, neither shall the trees of the land yield their fruits [Lev. 26:18–20].**

This is the second degree of judgment. If they were obdurate and continual in their disobedience, then God would judge them seven times, which indicates a complete and absolute judgment. Their pride would be broken. There would be no rain; there would be continual crop failure.

> **And if ye walk contrary unto me, and will not hearken unto me; I will bring seven times more plagues upon you according to your sins.**
>
> **I will also send wild beasts among you, which shall rob you of your children, and destroy your cattle, and make you few in number; and your high ways shall be desolate [Lev. 26:21–22].**

This is the third degree judgment. Plagues and wild beasts will decimate the population. All of this came upon them. Read in Judges where they traveled on the byways while the highways were unoccupied. Man has lost his dominion over nature.

> **And if ye will not be reformed by me by these things, but will walk contrary unto me;**
>
> **Then will I also walk contrary unto you, and will punish you yet seven times for your sins.**

> And I will bring a sword upon you, that shall avenge the quarrel of my covenant: and when ye are gathered together within your cities, I will send the pestilence among you; and ye shall be delivered into the hand of the enemy.

> And when I have broken the staff of your bread, ten women shall bake your bread in one oven, and they shall deliver you your bread again by weight: and ye shall eat and not be satisfied [Lev. 26:23–26].

This is the fourth degree judgment. Notice the repetition of the number seven, which indicates completeness. The enemy will breach their defenses, and the pestilence will strike the people. Captivity would be the end result.

Ezekiel warned them that a third part would die of the pestilence and with famine, a third part would be scattered (Ezek. 5:12). Isaiah, Jeremiah, and Ezekiel all warned them of famine which would overtake them. It all happened.

This will take place again at the time of the Great Tribulation, as we find it in the sixth chapter of the Book of Revelation.

> And if ye will not for all this hearken unto me, but walk contrary unto me;

> Then I will walk contrary unto you also in fury; and I, even I, will chastise you seven times for your sins.

> And ye shall eat the flesh of your sons, and the flesh of your daughters shall ye eat [Lev. 26:27–29].

This seems terribly harsh, and one would think it could never come to pass. But it did.

> And I will destroy your high places, and cut down your images, and cast your carcases upon the carcases of your idols, and my soul shall abhor you.

> And I will make your cities waste, and bring your sanctuaries unto desolation, and I will not smell the savour of your sweet odours.
>
> And I will bring the land into desolation: and your enemies which dwell therein shall be astonished at it.
>
> And I will scatter you among the heathen, and will draw out a sword after you: and your land shall be desolate, and your cities waste [Lev. 26:30–33].

This is the fifth degree judgment, and it is extreme. It was the result of warfare in the siege of the cities. This was fulfilled in the siege of Samaria (2 Kings 6:28–29), and again in the siege of Jerusalem by the Babylonians under Nebuchadnezzar (Lam. 2:20; 4:10), and again when Titus the Roman attacked Jerusalem in A.D. 70. Verse 33 is a picture of the land as it stood for 1900 years. God does what He says He will do.

> Then shall the land enjoy her sabbaths, as long as it lieth desolate, and ye be in your enemies' land; even then shall the land rest, and enjoy her sabbaths.
>
> As long as it lieth desolate it shall rest; because it did not rest in your sabbaths, when ye dwelt upon it [Lev. 26:34–35].

Here is the reason they went into the Babylonian captivity. During 490 years Israel failed to give the land its Sabbaths. That means the land missed seventy Sabbath years. The people of Israel thought they were getting by with it, but finally God said it was enough. If they wouldn't give the land its Sabbaths, God would. So He put them out of the land for seventy years. How accurate God is! This is why the Babylonian captivity lasted seventy years (2 Chron. 36:21).

> And upon them that are left alive of you I will send a faintness into their hearts in the lands of their enemies;

and the sound of a shaken leaf shall chase them; and they shall flee, as fleeing from a sword; and they shall fall when none pursueth.

And they shall fall one upon another, as it were before a sword, when none pursueth: and ye shall have no power to stand before your enemies.

And ye shall perish among the heathen, and the land of your enemies shall eat you up.

And they that are left of you shall pine away in their iniquity in your enemies' lands; and also in the iniquities of their fathers shall they pine away with them [Lev. 26:36-39].

This is an accurate prophetic portrayal of the Jew since the days of the Babylonian captivity, as he has been scattered among the nations. Wave after wave of anti-Semitism has descended upon him to destroy him. This section is a striking picture of the Nazi anti-Semitic movement. You can see that this Book of Leviticus is up-to-date.

PREDICTION PREDICATED
ON PROMISE TO PATRIARCHS

If they shall confess their iniquity, and the iniquity of their fathers, with their trespass which they trespassed against me, and that also they have walked contrary unto me;

And that I also have walked contrary unto them, and have brought them into the land of their enemies; if then their uncircumcised hearts be humbled, and they then accept of the punishment of their iniquity:

Then will I remember my covenant with Jacob, and also my covenant with Isaac, and also my covenant with Abraham will I remember; and I will remember the land [Lev. 26:40-42].

All of their past iniquity does not destroy the fact that Israel holds the title deed to that land. This is a remarkable prophecy and one that God says He will fulfill when the time has come. God will not utterly destroy them because of His covenant with Abraham and other patriarchs. We found in the Book of Exodus that when Israel was in slavery in Egypt, God heard their groaning, God remembered His covenant with Abraham, Isaac, and Jacob, and so God delivered them out of Egypt (Exod. 2:24–25).

Now God tells them they can stay in the land if they will obey Him. If not, they must leave the land. But if they will repent and turn to God when they are out of the land, then He will bring them back into the land. So we find that Daniel turned to God in prayer when he was down in Babylon. He turned his face toward Jerusalem, he confessed his sins and the sins of his people, and when he did that, God heard. God sent a messenger to him to tell him they would return to the land. And they did return back to the land!

God still has a future purpose for the nation which the judgment of the past cannot nullify. Read Romans 11:1–25 and Jeremiah 31:31–34 in this connection.

> **The land also shall be left of them, and shall enjoy her sabbaths, while she lieth desolate without them: and they shall accept of the punishment of their iniquity: because, even because they despised my judgments, and because their soul abhorred my statutes.**
>
> **And yet for all that, when they be in the land of their enemies, I will not cast them away, neither will I abhor them, to destroy them utterly, and to break my covenant with them: for I am the LORD their God [Lev. 26:43–44].**

This is a remarkable passage of Scripture. Can you say that God is through with the nation Israel after you have read this passage? If you believe that God means what He says, then He is not through with them at all.

But I will for their sakes remember the covenant of their ancestors, whom I brought forth out of the land of Egypt in the sight of the heathen, that I might be their God: I am the LORD.

These are the statutes and judgments and laws, which the LORD made between him and the children of Israel in mount Sinai by the hand of Moses [Lev. 26:45–46].

They brought judgment upon Palestine just as Adam brought judgment upon the whole earth by his sin. Because of God's covenant with their fathers, He will return them to the land and restore all that He had promised to them.

We have come to the end of the giving of these laws here in Leviticus. God confirms the Pentateuch here as given through Moses. This verse seems to end the book, but it doesn't.

God looks down through the ages to their repeated failures and His faithfulness and final victory. Moses could not bring them eternal blessings, although he was a mediator. The world must look to Another. John gives us the answer: "For the law was given by Moses, but grace and truth came by Jesus Christ" (John 1:17).

CHAPTER 27

THEME: Commutation of vows concerning persons; commutation of vows concerning animals; commutation of vows concerning houses; commutation of vows concerning land; concerning three things which are the Lord's apart from a vow

When you begin to read this chapter, you wonder why it is here. It seems to be an addendum or a postscript to the Book of Leviticus. All the expositors note this, and some actually consider this a major problem of the book. J. A. Seiss doesn't include it with the Book of Leviticus, and Dr. Langley treats it as an appendix. Although the subject matter seems to be extraneous and unrelated to the contents of the book, I see no reason to make a mountain out of a molehill.

I think there is a definite purpose in placing this chapter last. Dr. S. H. Kellogg notes with real spiritual perception that what has preceded this chapter is obligatory, while this is voluntary. Actually, this makes a beautiful and fitting climax to the book of worship.

In much this same way, chapter 21 of John's Gospel follows the climax of chapter 20. In chapter 20 the risen Lord has revealed Himself to His disciples and has sent them out into the world. But wait a minute—He has a message to Simon Peter in chapter 21, "If you love me, feed my sheep." It is voluntary, and the basis for it is love. That is God's method.

A striking feature about the vows is that they are voluntary. They follow the commandments, ceremonies, and ordinances. It is going the second mile after God has required the first mile. They are the response of a grateful heart. However, it is important to note that after a promise has been made to God, it is essential that it be fulfilled.

The natural response of a saved person is to ask what he can do for the Lord since the Lord has done so much for him. We find this expressed many times in the Scripture. "What shall I render unto the

LORD for all his benefits toward me?" (Ps. 116:12). The apostle Paul wrote to the believers of his day, "I beseech you therefore, brethren, by the mercies of God, that ye present your bodies a living sacrifice, holy, acceptable unto God, which is your reasonable service" (Rom. 12:1). This is not a command. He says, "I *beseech* you." In Titus 2:11 he wrote, "For the grace of God that bringeth salvation hath appeared to all men." What does it do? Does it demand something? No. "Teaching us that, denying ungodliness and worldly lusts, we should live soberly, righteously, and godly, in this present world" (Titus 2:12). Micah evidently had this chapter in mind when he wrote, "He hath shewed thee, O man, what is good; and what does the LORD require of thee, but to do justly, and to love mercy, and to walk humbly with thy God?" (Mic. 6:8).

Every normal believer wants to do something for God. He wants to pledge something to God. The deepest problem is to find something worthy to pledge to God. Ephraim Syrus wrote, "I pronounce my life wretched, because it is unprofitable." David Brainerd cried, "O that my soul were holy as He is holy! O that it were pure as Christ is pure, and perfect as my Father in Heaven is perfect! These are the sweetest commands in God's book, comprising all others. And shall I break them? Must I break them? Am I under a necessity of it as long as I live in the world? O my soul! woe, woe is me that I am a sinner." What can a saved sinner offer to God? This chapter answers that question.

Once a vow was made, it became mandatory. "It is a snare to the man who devoureth that which is holy, and after vows to make enquiry" (Prov. 20:25). You make the inquiry first so you know what you are doing. "When thou vowest a vow unto God, defer not to pay it; for he hath no pleasure in fools: pay that which thou hast vowed. Better is it that thou shouldest not vow, than that thou shouldest vow and not pay. Suffer not thy mouth to cause thy flesh to sin; neither say thou before the angel, that it was an error: wherefore should God be angry at thy voice, and destroy the work of thine hands?" (Eccl. 5:4–6).

There were promissory vows and there were vows of renunciation. These vows figured large in the life of the nation. Then there was the Nazarite vow which is given in detail in Numbers 6. The most notable vow is the one made by Jephthah. "And Jephthah vowed a vow unto the LORD, and said, If thou shalt without fail deliver the children of Ammon into mine hands, then it shall be, that whatsoever cometh forth of the doors of my house to meet me, when I return in peace from the children of Ammon, shall surely be the LORD's, and I will offer it up for a burnt offering" (Judg. 11:30–31). We know that God strictly forbade human sacrifice. I believe the original can also be translated, ". . . when I return in peace from the children of Ammon, shall surely be the LORD's, or I will offer up a burnt offering." Remember that it was his daughter who ran out to greet him. He did not sacrifice his daughter, but he did offer her up to the Lord. This is made clear in Judges 11:39–40: "And it came to pass at the end of two months, that she returned unto her father, who did with her according to his vow which he had vowed: and she knew no man. And it was a custom in Israel, that the daughters of Israel went yearly to lament the daughter of Jephthah the Gileadite four days in a year." In other words, she did not marry. For a Hebrew woman, this was a terrible thing. She was dedicated wholly to the Lord. Jephthah offered her to the Lord, but he did not sacrifice her by killing her.

It was a rash vow that he had made, but at least he kept it. If a vow was not kept, a trespass and sin offering must be made (Lev. 5:4–6).

I believe that God will hold you to your vow. A great many Christians today are not keeping their vows to God. If you do not intend to keep a vow, or you think lightly about your dealing with God, then you had better take a second look at it. I think that there are many Christians who have been set aside today. There are many who are being judged and many who have fallen asleep as Paul says. Remember, God is not asking you to make a vow. It is voluntary. But if you do promise God something, be sure you go through with it. "When thou shalt vow a vow unto the LORD thy God, thou shalt not slack to pay it: for the LORD thy God will surely require it of thee; and it would be sin in thee. But if thou shalt forbear to vow, it shall be no sin in thee. That which is gone out of thy lips thou shalt keep and perform; even a freewill offering, according as thou has vowed unto the LORD thy God, which thou hast promised with thy mouth" (Deut. 23:21–23).

COMMUTATION OF VOWS CONCERNING PERSONS

And the LORD spake unto Moses, saying,

Speak unto the children of Israel, and say unto them, When a man shall make a singular vow, the persons shall be for the LORD by thy estimation [Lev. 27:1–2].

"Making a singular vow," means to single out something of value, particularly precious to the individual. Remember how David would not offer to God something which had been donated to him. ". . . Nay; but I will surely buy it of thee at a price: neither will I offer burnt offerings unto the LORD my God of that which doth cost me nothing . . ." (2 Sam. 24:24).

If you are in a church and you are attempting to give to God some offering that costs you nothing, may God have mercy on you! We are not under a tithe system today. Israel was, but we are not. God does not require a tithe of us. We are to give a freewill offering. I can promise you that if you are cheap with God, God will be cheap with you.

A successful business man was asked the secret of his success. He said, "As the Lord shovels it in, I shovel it out; the more I shovel it out, the more the Lord shovels it in." Now, that is not to say that the Lord is promising to bless us with money. He has many kinds of blessings for us. However, I do believe that some of us are poor today and some of us have such a hard time financially because of the way we deal with God.

A man came to me when the stock market crashed, and he brought in some stock which he offered with this comment, "Now that it is going down, I might just as well give it to the church." God have mercy on that kind of giving. We are to give something of value. It should cost us something.

And thy estimation shall be of the male from twenty years old even unto sixty years old, even thy estimation shall be fifty shekels of silver, after the shekel of the sanctuary.

And if it be a female, then thy estimation shall be thirty shekels [Lev. 27:3–4].

When a person was dedicated by a vow to God, it did not mean that individual must serve in the tabernacle—that was the peculiar service of the Levites. A redemption price could be paid for the person which would relieve him of that service. This is called the commutation price of the person.

A man between the ages of twenty and sixty was of greater value because of the amount of work he could do. The labor value seemed to be the standard of evaluation. A male in the prime of life could render the most service. "By thy estimation" meant that which was the current value among the people.

The labor value of a female would be less, but the important feature is that a female could be devoted to God. I think this makes it clear that the daughter of Jephthah was not offered as a human sacrifice but remained unmarried and was vowed to God.

Hannah brought little Samuel to the temple as a thanksgiving offering to God in payment of her vow. She said, "For this child I prayed; and the LORD hath given me my petition which I asked of him: Therefore also I have lent him to the LORD; as long as he liveth he shall be lent to the LORD . . ." (1 Sam. 1:27–28). She kept her vow.

Have you ever come to God and presented yourself to Him? Have you presented your children to God? Your grandchildren? Have you presented your possessions to Him? He hasn't commanded you to do that, but He has said that you may do it. If you do it, then it is mandatory that you make good.

And if it be from five years old even unto twenty years old, then thy estimation shall be of the male twenty shekels, and for the female ten shekels.

And if it be from a month old even unto five years old, then thy estimation shall be of the male five shekels of silver, and for the female thy estimation shall be three shekels of silver.

> And if it be from sixty years old and above; if it be a male, then thy estimation shall be fifteen shekels, and for the female ten shekels.
>
> But if he be poorer than thy estimation, then he shall present himself before the priest, and the priest shall value him; according to his ability that vowed shall the priest value him [Lev. 27:5-8].

You see that the scale of values was determined by age and not by social position, riches, or prestige. The value was based on the ability to labor. Notice how wonderfully God provided for the poor so they could participate in this voluntary service. A fair and equitable price was set by the priest according to the man's ability to pay. The widow's mite is of more value in heaven than the rich gifts of the wealthy and affluent.

There is another striking feature about the vowing of persons. Ordinarily in human affairs, a man pays for the service of another. In the law of vows this is reversed and a man pays to serve God. It is a privilege to serve God.

COMMUTATION OF VOWS CONCERNING ANIMALS

> And if it be a beast, whereof men bring an offering unto the LORD, all that any man giveth of such unto the LORD shall be holy.
>
> He shall not alter it, nor change it, a good for a bad, or a bad for a good: and if he shall at all change beast for beast, then it and the exchange thereof shall be holy [Lev. 27:9-10].

When I was pastor of a little country church, a member of the church took me out to his barn lot and showed me a calf. He told me he had given it to the LORD. To tell you the truth, that calf didn't look as if it would live, and I suspect that is the reason he gave it to the Lord. Well, that calf became a blue-ribbon prize winner! Then the man told me,

"You know, this is such a fine animal that I thought I'd better keep it. I have another animal over here that I'm giving to the Lord instead." He sold it and gave the money to the church, and felt very comfortable about what he had done.

God says, "Don't substitute." If you have promised to do something for God, go through with it. Remember the sin of Ananias and Sapphira. They said they were giving to the Lord the entire price of a piece of land, but they didn't go through with it. They didn't have to give all of it to God. Peter told them that while it was theirs, they were perfectly free to do with it what they wished. It was a voluntary offering, but then they tried to withhold some of it from God.

This that we are talking about is real today. God holds us to our vows. If you have promised Him something and haven't made good, it is still on His books. We are dealing with a God of reality.

And if it be any unclean beast, of which they do not offer a sacrifice unto the LORD then he shall present the beast before the priest:

And the priest shall value it, whether it be good or bad: as thou valuest it, who art the priest, so shall it be.

But if he will at all redeem it, then he shall add a fifth part thereof unto thy estimation [Lev. 27:11–13].

An unclean animal could be pledged in a vow, but it would not be offered in sacrifice. The priest would value the animal, the man would pay the price of redemption and add a fifth of the price as a sort of fine for offering an unclean animal.

COMMUTATION OF VOWS CONCERNING HOUSES

And when a man shall sanctify his house to be holy unto the LORD, then the priest shall estimate it, whether it be good or bad; as the priest shall estimate it, so shall it stand.

And if he that sanctified it will redeem his house, then he shall add the fifth part of the money of thy estimation unto it, and it shall be his [Lev. 27:14–15].

The home of a man is his most sacred material possession. He could pledge it to the Lord. I think a Christian home, as well as the children of Christians, should be dedicated to God. The man could continue to live in his house and begin paying rent to God as the owner. If he did not continue paying his rent, he was to add a fifth when he redeemed it. Again this was a sort of fine in recognition of God's ownership.

A man asked me to come out to dedicate his house. He said he wanted it to be God's house, and I could come out there any time I wanted to. Well, I had a house of my own and didn't need to be running out to his house. If he really meant that it was God's house, then he should pay God rent for it as a recognition of God's ownership. You may ask me whether I think this is that literal. Yes, I think it is just that literal. We make vows to God of our freewill. Then we prove whether or not we are genuine in our vows. This gets right down to the nitty-gritty where you and I live.

COMMUTATION OF VOWS CONCERNING LAND

And if a man shall sanctify unto the Lord some part of a field of his possession, then thy estimation shall be according to the seed thereof: an homer of barley seed shall be valued at fifty shekels of silver.

If he sanctify his field from the year of jubile, according to thy estimation it shall stand.

But if he sanctify his field after the jubile, then the priest shall reckon unto him the money according to the years that remain, even unto the year of the jubile, and it shall be abated from thy estimation.

And if he that sanctified the field will in any wise redeem it, then he shall add the fifth part of the money of thy estimation unto it, and it shall be assured to him.

And if he will not redeem the field, or if he have sold the field to another man, it shall not be redeemed any more.

But the field, when it goeth out in the jubile, shall be holy unto the LORD, as a field devoted; the possession thereof shall be the priest's.

And if a man sanctify unto the LORD a field which he hath bought, which is not of the fields of his possession;

Then the priest shall reckon unto him the worth of thy estimation, even unto the year of the jubile: and he shall give thine estimation in that day, as a holy thing unto the LORD.

In the year of the jubile the field shall return unto him of whom it was bought, even to him to whom the possession of the land did belong.

And all thy estimations shall be according to the shekel of the sanctuary: twenty gerahs shall be the shekel [Lev. 27:16–25].

This must have been a very complicated system. Land could be dedicated to God even though the land belonged to God. The land was evaluated on the basis of its productivity and in relation to the year of Jubilee. All land returned to the original owner at that time. This was taken into account if a man dedicated the land to the Lord just shortly before the year of Jubilee as a gesture of generosity. In fact he might be a very selfish man. A man could not dedicate a borrowed field to God. God knows the heart of man.

CONCERNING THREE THINGS WHICH ARE THE LORD'S APART FROM A VOW

Only the firstling of the beasts, which should be the LORD's firstling, no man shall sanctify it; whether it be ox, or sheep: it is the LORD's.

> And if it be of an unclean beast, then he shall redeem it according to thine estimation, and shall add a fifth part of it thereto: or if it be not redeemed, then it shall be sold according to thy estimation [Lev. 27:26–27].

The firstborn of both man and beast were already claimed by the Lord and could not be devoted to the Lord in a vow. God insisted that His rights be observed.

> Notwithstanding no devoted thing, that a man shall devote unto the LORD of all that he hath, both of man and beast, and of the field of his possession, shall be sold or redeemed: every devoted thing is most holy unto the LORD.

> None devoted, which shall be devoted of men, shall be redeemed; but shall surely be put to death [Lev. 27:28–29].

The second classification of things which could not be devoted in a vow was that which was already pledged in a vow to God. In Joshua we learn that Jericho was devoted to God for destruction. Because Achan took of that which God had told them they should utterly destroy, Achan was destroyed (Josh. 6 and 7).

> And all the tithe of the land, whether of the seed of the land, or of the fruit of the tree, is the LORD's: it is holy unto the LORD.

> And if a man will at all redeem aught of his tithes, he shall add thereto the fifth part thereof.

> And concerning the tithe of the herd, or of the flock, even of whatsoever passeth under the rod, the tenth shall be holy unto the LORD.

> He shall not search whether it be good or bad, neither shall he change it: and if he change it at all, then both it

**and the change thereof shall be holy; it shall not be re-
deemed [Lev. 27:30–33].**

The tithe was the third thing which already belonged to God and
could not be pledged in a vow.

**These are the commandments, which the LORD com-
manded Moses for the children of Israel in mount Sinai
[Lev. 27:34].**

This verse concludes the Book of Leviticus and sums it up. It also
reveals that chapter 27 is not an addendum but part and parcel of the
thinking of God for man under law.

The believer can be thankful for the grace of God in this day. "For
the grace of God that bringeth salvation hath appeared to all men,
Teaching us that, denying ungodliness and worldly lusts, we should
live soberly, righteously, and godly, in this present world; looking for
that blessed hope, and the glorious appearing of the great God and our
Saviour Jesus Christ; Who gave himself for us, that he might redeem
us from all iniquity, and purify unto himself a peculiar people, zeal-
ous of good works" (Titus 2:11–14).

BIBLIOGRAPHY
(Recommended for Further Study)

Gaebelein, Arno C. *Annotated Bible*, Vol. 1. Neptune, New Jersey: Loizeaux Brothers, 1917.

Goldberg, Louis. *Leviticus*. Grand Rapids, Michigan: Zondervan Publishing House, 1980.

Grant, F. W. *Numerical Bible*. Neptune, New Jersey: Loizeaux Brothers, 1891.

Gray, James M. *Synthetic Bible Studies*. Westwood, New Jersey: Fleming H. Revell Co., 1906.

Heslop, W. G. *Lessons from Leviticus*. Grand Rapids, Michigan: Kregel Publications, 1945.

Ironside, H. A. *Lectures on the Levitical Offerings*. Neptune, New Jersey: Loizeaux Brothers, 1929.

Jamieson, Robert; Faucett, H. R.; and Brown, D. *Commentary on the Bible*. 3 vols. Grand Rapids, Michigan: Wm. B. Eerdmans Publishing Co., 1945.

Jensen, Irving L. *Leviticus*. Chicago, Illinois: Moody Press, 1967.

Jukes, Andrew. *The Law of the Offerings*. Grand Rapids, Michigan: Kregel Publications, 1870.

Kellogg, S. H. *The Book of Leviticus*. New York: George H. Doran Co., 1908.

Kelly, William. *Lectures Introductory to the Pentateuch*. Oak Park, Illinois: Bible Truth Publishers, 1870.

Mackintosh, C. H. (C.H.M.). *Notes on the Pentateuch*. Neptune, New Jersey: Loizeaux Brothers, 1880.

McGee, J. Vernon. *Learning Through Leviticus*. 2 vols. Pasadena, California: Thru the Bible Books, 1964.

Noordtzij, A. *Leviticus*. Grand Rapids, Michigan: Zondervan Publishing House, 1982.

Slemming, C. W. *These are the Garments*. London, England: Marshall Morgan & Scott, n.d.

Slemming, C. W. *Thus Shalt Thou Serve*. Fort Washington, Pennsylvania: Christian Literature Crusade, 1955.

Shultz, Samuel J. *Leviticus*. Chicago, Illinois: Moody Press, 1983.

Thomas, W. H. Griffith. *Through the Pentateuch Chapter by Chapter*. Grand Rapids, Michigan: Wm. B. Eerdmans Publishing Co., 1957.

Unger, Merrill F. *Unger's Bible Handbook*. Chicago, Illinois: Moody Press, 1966.

Unger, Merrill F. *Unger's Commentary on the Old Testament*, Vol. I. Chicago, Illinois: Moody Press, 1981.